insight text guide

Timothy Derricourt

The Turning

Tim Winton

First published in 2023.

Insight Publications Pty Ltd
3/350 Charman Road
Cheltenham VIC 3192
Australia
Tel: +61 3 8571 4950
Fax: +61 3 8571 0257
Email: books@insightpublications.com.au

www.insightpublications.com.au

A catalogue record for this book is available from the National Library of Australia

Tim Winton's The Turning / Timothy Derricourt

Timothy Derricourt asserts the moral right to be identified as the author of this work.

ISBNs:
9781923016279 (print)
9781923016286 (digital)
9781923016293 (bundle: print + digital)

Cover design by Hayley Sinnatt

Printed by Markono Print Media Pte Ltd

contents

CHARACTER MAP

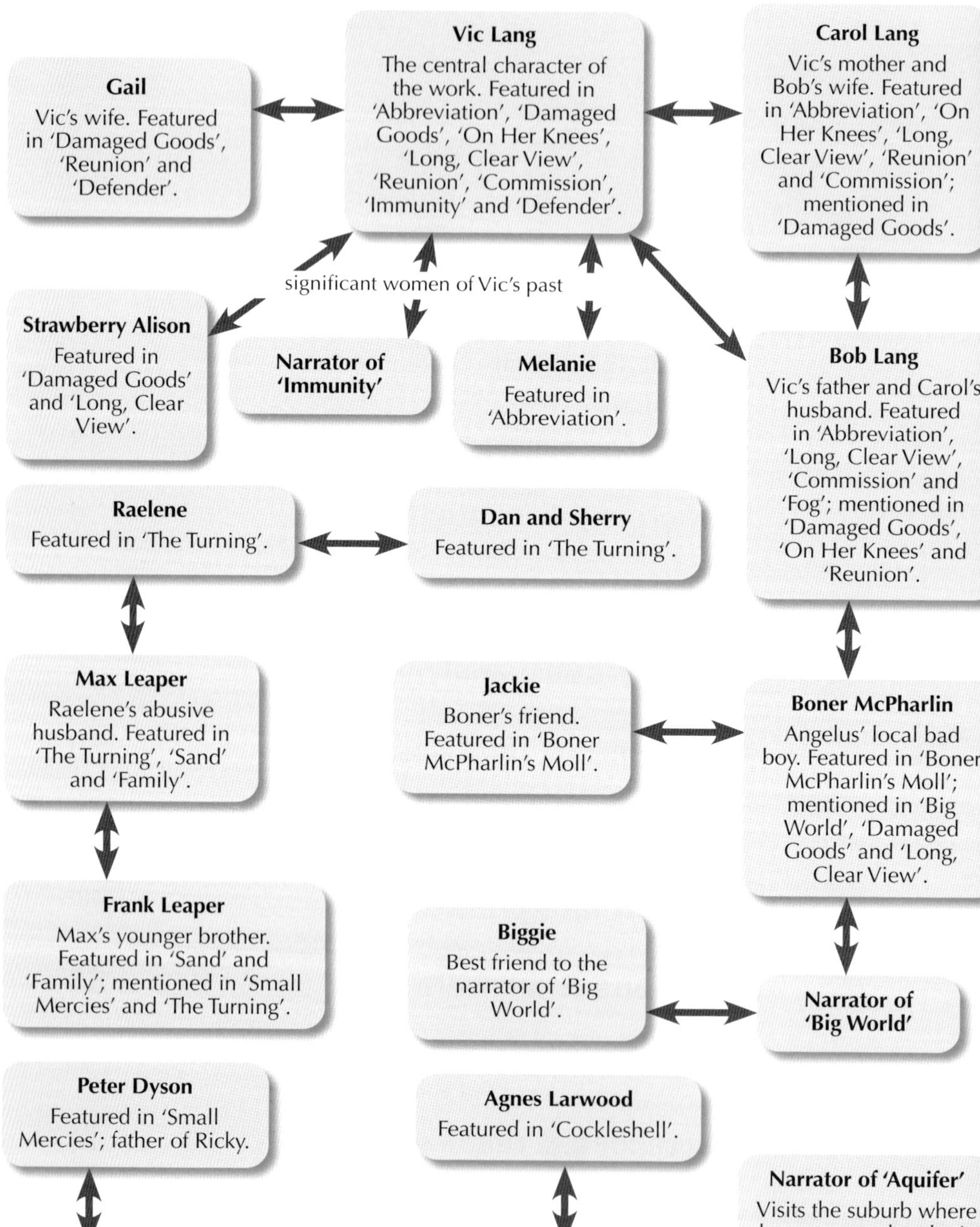

OVERVIEW

About the author

Tim Winton is perhaps the defining voice of Australian literature. A prolific writer, a passionate ecologist and a famously reclusive figure, he has cemented his place both in the global literary canon and as a spokesperson on Australian culture, identity and environment, with more than thirty works of celebrated fiction and nonfiction.

Winton was born on 4 August 1960, in Perth, Western Australia. At the age of twelve he moved with his family from the Perth suburb of Karrinyup to the rugged whaling town of Albany, on Western Australia's south-west coast, where he lived for three years. The son of a local police officer, raised in a working-class, evangelical family, Winton found himself drawn to writing from a young age, despite the pull towards the life of trade that characterised his community. His early life had a profound impact on his writing, much of which is grounded in autobiographical detail. He found solace in the natural environment, and he has remained firmly attached to the geography of his upbringing, living and working – at the same desk on which he wrote his first pieces – immersed in the beauty and harshness of the Western Australian coastline.

Winton was studying at the Western Australian Institute of Technology (now Curtin University, which has a building named for him) when he wrote his first novel, *An Open Swimmer* (1982). Released when he was just twenty-two, the novel won the *Australian*/Vogel Literary Award and launched his career as an author. Since then, Winton's literary star has never faded. He won the Miles Franklin Award for *Shallows* (1984), *Cloudstreet* (1991), *Dirt Music* (2002) and *Breath* (2009) and was nominated for the internationally prestigious Booker Prize for *The Riders* (1994) and *Dirt Music*.

Cloudstreet has become one of the definitive Australian novels of the last century, a magnum opus set in a dilapidated house in Perth and exploring core Australian themes of familial bonds, individual hardiness and raffish qualities that epitomise the enduring Australian spirit. *The Turning*, Winton's collection of interwoven short stories, was the winner of the Christina Stead Prize and the Queensland Premier's Best Fiction Book. It has been adapted into a film starring, among others, Cate Blanchett, Hugo Weaving and Rose Byrne.

In a literary world that sees few writers succeed beyond more than a handful of works, Winton has remained a beloved and acclaimed literary great in Australia. His novels (and more recently his nonfiction) consistently find new and vital ways to represent Australia's complex cultural identity for ever-expanding global audiences.

Winton is equally well known for his unyielding environmental activism, and he was awarded the 2003 Australian Society of Authors Medal for his advocacy. He has lent his powerful voice to a range of environmental causes, writing of the need to conserve the Australian wilderness in his many essays and in his collected works of nonfiction, *Island Home* (2015) and *The Boy Behind the Curtain* (2016). He was instrumental in the prominent Save Ningaloo Campaign, which saw the Ningaloo Reef gain National Heritage status. The three-part ABC series *Ningaloo Nyinggulu* (2023) captures his love and care for the region.

In 2023, Winton was awarded the Lloyd O'Neil Award for outstanding service to the Australian book industry and was made an officer of the Order of Australia as part of the King's Birthday Honours List.

Synopsis

The Turning is a collection of seventeen interconnected short stories largely set around the fictional coastal town of Angelus, Western Australia, inspired by Winton's own upbringing in the whaling town of Albany. Winton offers snapshots into the lives of a collection of individuals struggling to survive in a harsh and unforgiving community while simultaneously seeking understanding, escape and closure. Starting in the early 1970s and ending in the early 2000s, the stories focus on the experiences of various families, teenagers and social outsiders: two boys on a road trip celebrating the end of high school discover the escape is not all they thought it would be; two brothers, bitterly feuding, find themselves needing to work together during a shark attack; a young mother attempts to find salvation when faced with the reality of a violent husband.

While many of the stories are seemingly disconnected, Winton uses the nonlinear narrative structure to skilfully weave threads that bind the individuals together and expose the fragility of human connections. Central to the work is the character arc of Vic Lang, whom we follow from adolescence into adulthood in a series of leaps in time. Through his story, and many of the others, Winton seeks to show how individuals must grapple with their past experiences and the regrets that haunt them to embark on a journey of redemption and closure and seek personal transformation, or a 'turning'. Surrounding the individual human stories are the landscape and community themselves; almost characters in their own right. The rugged harshness of the Australian coast and wilderness reflect and even liberate the characters from the struggles they face. Despite the bleak nature of the collection, Winton ultimately portrays the hope and salvation possible for those who seek them.

Character summaries

Vic Lang

The central character of the collection, whom we follow from adolescence to adulthood, when he is coming to terms with his past.

Gail

Vic's wife, who is desperately trying to piece together Vic's past while struggling to maintain her relationship with him.

Carol Lang

Vic's mother, whom we meet at various stages of her life, including as a young mother and later as a cleaner, after her husband leaves her.

Bob Lang

Vic's father, a policeman, who is unable to tolerate the corruption in the police force in Angelus and becomes dependent on alcohol. We later meet him living a reclusive, sober life in the outback.

Frank Leaper

The younger Leaper brother, who has a successful but brief career as an Australian Football League star, then walks away from it, haunted by his unresolved family issues.

Max Leaper

The older Leaper brother, a violent and cruel man, married to Raelene and ceaselessly bitter about his failed life.

Raelene

A young mother of two and the violently abused wife of Max Leaper. She finds hope in the kindness of new friends Dan and Sherry and their religious perspective on life.

Boner McPharlin

The local Angelus bad boy, who becomes involved in drug dealing and ends up a broken and disturbed man.

Jackie

Depicted as both a young teen and as an adult; troubled by her relationship with Boner and her failure as a friend.

Peter Dyson

A father grieving the death of his wife, who returns to Angelus to raise his young son in a new environment but becomes reluctantly re-immersed in a past relationship and its unresolved damage.

Fay Keenan

Peter's high-school girlfriend, who had an abortion when she was 'two days shy of seventeen' (p.98) and is struggling to bring up a daughter while trying to remain free of drugs.

Agnes Larwood

A fifteen-year-old girl living in Cockleshell who escapes her family dramas by fishing and, ultimately, when her father dies in a house fire.

Brakey

A fifteen-year-old boy living in Cockleshell who for a short time is obsessed with Agnes.

BACKGROUND & CONTEXT

Historical setting

Published in 2004, *The Turning* alludes to historical events of the period from the 1970s to the turn of the century. These elements provide some background context to the book's stories.

Australian culture and society

Broadly, the stories are best understood within their Australian context. With Esso petrol stations, blockout, Holdens and Corollas, and jargon such as 'chick magnets', 'friggen' and 'old farts', Winton leans in to, and critically examines, the cultural qualities that define a particular white, small-town Australia that idolises masculine strength and bravado, social conformity and a specific hardiness that has become a mainstay of Australian national identity. The 1970s particularly was an era of Australian nationhood growing away from the influence of England, which characterised earlier generations, and moving towards this brand of 'ocker' cultural identity that still exists today and is highlighted in Winton's many works of fiction.

The stories also seem to reflect a change in Australian society, from a somewhat egalitarian country to one in which divisions between rich and poor are more prevalent. In 'Aquifer', the narrator's ironic comment that 'everyone's middle class in this country now' (p.52) reveals an underlying lack of belief in genuine social mobility (especially given the class within which most characters find themselves remaining) and reflects Winton's thoughts on the subject in some of his other works. These ideas are best expressed in his essay 'Using the C-Word', regarding the shift in Australia towards neoliberalism from the late 1990s, in which Winton senses class:

> grinding away tectonically in the experiences of relatives and friends, who may not want to talk about class but who are subject to its force every day. (Winton 2016, p.226)

Vietnam, Afghanistan and Iraq wars

In the background of the 1970s stories are the events of the Vietnam War. While Winton doesn't comment on the war itself, it serves as a useful juxtaposition to the violence of the town and its people, with Gail even explaining Vic's possible early violent tendencies in terms of the influence of 'Vietnam in shrieking flames on TV every night' ('Damaged Goods', p.58). As the stories move forward, a 'new war' ('Immunity', p.298) is mentioned, possibly the war in Afghanistan (which began in 2001) or in Iraq (beginning in 2003). Again, while Winton does not comment on the war, it is interesting to see his exploration of a fractured and violent society amid a broader global context of ongoing warfare and conflict.

Colonisation and reconciliation

Winton has made outspoken comments on First Nations issues in his nonfiction writings. In *The Turning*, while not placing it centrally, he alludes to the cultural history of dispossession and colonisation that has defined relations between First Nations peoples and non-Indigenous Australians. In stories such as 'Aquifer', 'Long, Clear View' and 'Defender', readers can identify issues of historical trauma, regret and unease that mark this disquieting relationship underpinning Australian society.

Author's context

Perhaps more significant than the book's historical setting is an understanding of Winton's biographical and cultural context. Winton's work can be read as an examination of Australian identity and culture, a culture that he himself was brought up within and both idolises and critiques.

His collection of nonfiction essays *The Boy Behind the Curtain* (2016) reveals much of the autobiographical detail that is included in *The Turning*, and there are striking similarities to Winton's own life when we compare the essays with the stories. Like Winton's father, Vic's father is a local policeman and faces challenges in his small community that impact his family. Stories such as 'Commission', 'Fog' and even 'Boner

McPharlin's Moll' are informed by Winton's inside understanding of the dark side of small-town Australia.

Winton also captures a feeling of being an outsider in such communities, reflecting his own alienation when he moved towns in his youth. In fact, the story 'Long, Clear View' is a direct re-telling of an event that Winton experienced himself: standing at the window of his house holding the family gun, watching 'the strangers of your town take their dirty secrets from place to place' ('Long, Clear View', p.204).

Furthermore, Winton's religious upbringing informs the stories, although, apart from 'The Turning', they are not specifically religious. Winton's understanding of faith, salvation and the importance of community spring from his being raised within an evangelical family, even if that faith and sense of salvation, in these stories, never takes place in a church or formal religious context. In his essay 'Twice on Sundays', Winton discusses this influence, particularly how 'it was church that taught me the beauty and power of language' (Winton 2016, p.106).

Literary context

Winton has suggested that his mode of writing – telling a clear and realistic story situated in the Australian landscape – could be seen as dated, but he argues that conflict with and understanding of the landscape are still central to Australian art. In his essay 'The Island Seen and Felt', Winton writes, 'This is why, despite the postmodern and nearly post-physical age we live and work in, Australian writers and painters continue to obsess about landscape' (Winton 2015, p.20). In this regard, Winton's work can be seen as part of the wider mythologising of Australia's landscape found in works by Patrick White, Randolph Stow and Henry Lawson and by contemporaries such as Richard Flanagan, Kate Grenville and Robert Drewe.

In its short-story format, *The Turning* marked a slight departure from Winton's more usual long-form novels. Yet it still explores the same general themes that Winton has become known for. In both his fiction and his nonfiction collections, he explores, examines and critiques aspects of Australian life. Prior to *The Turning,* he wrote *Dirt Music,* an exploration of an affair set amid the rugged wilderness of Western Australia, and he followed *The Turning* with *Breath,* an exhilarating coming-of-age novel about a young surfer's experiences. Thus, *The Turning* can be seen as part of a series of works that use the experiences of ordinary Australians in everyday locations to explore broader universal experiences of love, loss, trauma and salvation.

GENRE, STRUCTURE & LANGUAGE

Genre

The Turning is a collection of interconnected short stories sharing common themes and characters. It is best defined as a work of contemporary Australian fiction, literary fiction or social realism. Winton's focus on the lives of ordinary Australians mainly from working-class backgrounds is part of a long history of Australian works that romanticise and represent the marginalised and the rabble-rousers, those who challenge society and those who are challenged by it. In this, his work fits within the genres and tropes of classic Australian storytelling by some of white Australia's earliest writers: Henry Lawson, Banjo Paterson and Dorothea Mackellar.

Winton has spoken of his desire to give a voice to the Australian working classes and to use language to elevate their experiences so that they can be read as powerful and significant (Nicols 2022). The language in *The Turning* is lyrical and evocative, and it fits within the stylistic qualities of literary fiction. In particular, Winton's depictions of landscape are lofty in style and make use of vivid imagery to convey the vastness, beauty and harshness of nature and thus elevate individuals' experiences within it. His depiction of the Australian landscape (and those struggling to survive within it) also reflects an Australian literary genre that mythologises 'the bush', from the works of Patrick White (who famously wrote in *Voss*, 'Everyone is still afraid … of this country, and will not say it') and Randolph Stow to those of Richard Flanagan, Murray Bail and Kate Grenville.

Structure

The stories within *The Turning* are presented in a nonlinear structure, with Winton changing time periods, characters and settings with each story. In this way, the work is a narrative puzzle, asking readers to figure out the order in which the events take place. For instance, the title piece of the collection, 'The Turning' explores the impact of Max's deplorable acts of domestic violence. The next story, 'Sand', goes back in time and depicts Max and Frank Leaper as children battling it out in the sand dunes on a fishing trip. 'Family' then jumps forward in time to show Max and Frank as adults, still engaged in a bitter feud. We thus start to piece together and understand the brothers' lives through reading about their experiences across time.

In structuring his work in this way, Winton does not simply wish to challenge his readers and avoid traditional, linear storytelling. The fragmented nature of the narrative cleverly reflects the broader themes of the work: as the individuals struggle to piece together the puzzles of their fragmented lives and pasts, so too do we, as readers, try to reconstruct moments of the past and make sense of who they are and who they might be if they face up to this past.

On another allegorical level, the fragmented and broken nature of the stories might also be read as a symbol of the fractured and fragmented nature of the community of Angelus itself. While the characters drift past each other in these stories, they rarely connect with each other in any meaningful manner. Winton is perhaps commenting on the way such communities fail to connect, to unify and to help each other out when individuals are struggling. It certainly makes those moments in the book when people do help others all the more remarkable.

If you enjoy piecing together the puzzle of the stories, skip over the list below, which is a summary of the book's chronology with regard to Vic's life and events concerning some of the other central characters.

- 'Big World', set in the year some of the characters finish high school (in the late 1970s)
- 'Abbreviation', set on New Year's Eve in 1972, when Vic is twelve and his family has 'just moved down south. Angelus' (p.25)
- 'Damaged Goods', set in the 2000s, with reflections on the 1970s and Vic's time in high school

- 'On Her Knees', set in around 1980, with Carol and Vic having moved back to Perth, and when Vic is twenty
- 'Long, Clear View', set in the early 1970s, soon after the family's move to Angelus (Vic is 'the new copper's kid', p.189)
- 'Reunion', set in the early 2000s, when Vic and Gail are adults
- 'Commission', set in the early 2000s, just prior to Carol's and Bob's deaths
- 'Fog', set in September 1973, when Bob Lang has been in Angelus for 'ten months' (p.273)
- 'Boner McPharlin's Moll', spanning from the early 1970s up to the early 2000s
- 'Immunity', set in the mid 1970s, when Vic is fifteen
- 'Defender', set in the early 2000s, after Vic's parents have died

Language

Australian voice

Winton writes with a distinctly Australian voice, using colloquialism and the vernacular to capture a particularly authentic, small-town, white Australian tone. He shows great warmth towards the characters of everyday Australia and has done much to bring an Australian voice to a global audience. In fact, Winton has discussed his great efforts to hold out against foreign editors who have suggested toning down the Australian jargon for international audiences, suggesting that it is vital in understanding his particular depiction of life in Australia (The Royal Academy Podcast Team 2016). As you read through the book, pay close attention to the moments of colloquialism, jargon and clipped dialogue that reflect a very familiar Australian voice.

Symbolism

While all the stories contain authentically depicted characters, symbolism is crucial to an understanding of each work and should be central to an analysis of the ideas and themes at play in the text. Most importantly, the landscape and environment of each story play symbolic roles. From the breathtaking space the characters experience in 'Big World' and 'The Turning' to the confining township and scenery seen in 'Long, Clear View' and 'Fog', landscape serves to reflect the interior experiences of each character and to represent their emotional states.

Interestingly, the name Angelus has religious symbolism linked to the Catholic notion of the incarnation of God in the human form of Jesus. The work hints at the universal desire for some form of salvation, which many of the characters strive for as they attempt to piece together and save their broken lives and relationships.

Narrative point of view

The narrative point of view is an important aspect of the work. While a traditional novel often confines itself to one narrative perspective, this collection of short stories allows Winton to write from a range of perspectives. In addition, he skilfully plays with narrative point of view, employing shifts between first- and third-person storytelling, and even experimenting with the less common second-person perspective. This, much like the nonlinear structure, has a number of purposes. For one, we gain insight into varying points of view regarding life in small-town Australia (although collectively it all seems pretty bleak). Additionally, we see the same situations and characters from different angles and thus can form better, more objective pictures of them. In this, Winton encourages us to reconsider the subjective way in which we may see our own lives. He asks us to see them from a broader perspective if we seek to understand ourselves on a journey towards self-transformation.

STORY-BY-STORY ANALYSIS

Epigraph: extract from TS Eliot's 'Ash Wednesday'

Summary: *'Ash Wednesday' is a poem by modernist poet TS Eliot exploring themes of loss, faith and hope.*

In selecting an epigraph, Winton draws his reader's attention to some of the main ideas we can expect to encounter in *The Turning*. Firstly, the poem references the 'turning' of the book's title. In this instance, it indicates an ability to turn back towards the past or the desire to avoid such a turning. Ash Wednesday is a significant religious event of repentance (and the poem has been associated with Eliot's own conversion to Anglicanism), and thus the epigraph also hints at the search for redemption and closure that many of Winton's characters are engaged in. While the epigraph references religion (and Winton himself is a cautious believer), the stories do not focus on religion as a way of finding salvation, even if some of the characters do gain deeper spiritual awareness in their lives.

'Big World' (pp.1–15)

Summary: *Upon finishing high school, Biggie and the unnamed narrator work in an abattoir and save money in the hope of escaping their small-town lives. They eventually leave on an ill-fated road trip, and their friendship breaks apart.*

'Big World' is a stand-alone narrative, in that we don't meet Biggie or the narrator in the rest of the book. However, it introduces us to the town of Angelus and the major themes that develop through the rest of the work: coming of age, hope, escape, failure and trauma.

Key point

Coming of age can be an anticlimactic experience, especially when we find ourselves confined in the same world and values that we grew up with.

The story explores the anticlimactic nature of finishing high school and the way in which hopes and dreams, fostered through the years of being confined to school, might not be realised when school is finished. Being 'feverish with anticipation', the characters prepare themselves for 'a season of pandemonium' (p.1). However, Winton uses the symbolism of the landscape to foreshadow the dashing of such hopes. The 'southern sky presses down' (p.1), they accept low-skilled, low-paying jobs in the local meatworks, and they receive poor exam results.

The sense of claustrophobia and being 'anchored to the friggen place' (p.2) contrasts with the boys' dreams of escape into 'wide open spaces' (p.3). Thus, Winton portrays life in small-town Australia as one in which individuals can feel trapped: by expectations, by friendships and family, and by the limitations of their world.

When they hit the road, the two boys feel liberated, dreaming 'of the big world beyond' (p.6); yet, as the narrator notes, 'friendship ... comes at a price' (p.9). Despite their shared dreams, a chasm opens up between the two. The narrator – more intelligent and ambitious than Biggie – says, 'I'm stuck in something that I can't figure my way out of' (p.10).

A hitchhiker and a car fire later, it appears their hope of escape is dead. Despite the narrator's having felt on the precipice of a new life and at a turning point ('I really felt I'd reached the edge of something', p.12), the longed-for liberation from the old life is cut short.

Winton presents a seemingly cynical first story here, in which what we expect is not what we get. However, he is careful to depict the landscape in a positive manner, showing how, even through moments of havoc and difficulty, we can learn about ourselves and the world around us.

Key vocabulary

meatworks: an abattoir.

1967 Kombi, VW, Vee Dub: a camping van associated with the counterculture, hippy, surfing movement of the 1960s.

copper: a policeman.

Groucho Marx: a famous twentieth-century American comedian, part of the Marx Brothers siblings.

Lenny [Lennie] and George: characters from George Steinbeck's 1937 novella *Of Mice and Men*; George takes care of his friend Lennie, who has intellectual disability.

Skeleton Coast: an area of Namibia famed for its coastline littered with whalebones and abandoned ships.

Piazza San Marco: St Mark's Square, the main plaza in Venice.

Q As an introduction to the collection of stories, how does 'Big World' establish the culture and character of Angelus and life in small-town Australia?

Q While the boys' trip is a failure, the story ends with all three characters looking at a vast and beautiful landscape. What do you think is Winton's purpose in ending the story with this positive image?

'Abbreviation' (pp.17–36)

Summary: *Vic Lang, aged twelve, heads to White Point with his family for a holiday over New Year's Eve. While there, he meets Melanie, an older girl, with whom he has his first sexual encounter. On a fishing excursion, Vic falls overboard and gets a hook caught in his leg. When he goes back to look for Melanie, she and her family are gone.*

'Abbreviation' focuses on pain and injury and how these experiences are necessary parts of coming of age. The title itself suggests something missing, an absence. Specifically, it refers to the abbreviation of Melanie's finger, lost in a farming accident – a painful event that could be seen to be a traumatic turning point. On another level, the abbreviation is the cut-short experience Vic has with Melanie, in which he feels on the verge of something 'out of his reach, the way everything is when you're just a stupid kid' (p.33).

At the start of the story, Vic is depicted as an outcast in his own family, anxious and feeling the pressure of the world, waking from sleep 'certain the sea had overrun them' (p.19). His experience with Melanie seems to liberate him. Interestingly, Melanie aggressively pinches Vic's earlobe while kissing him, having just stated, 'All the big things hurt, the things you remember. If it doesn't hurt it's not important' (p.26). We see how this important turning point in Vic's life is simultaneously pleasurable and painful. The connection of pain with life-changing experiences is at the heart of *The Turning*, and it appears again and again through the range of characters who are transformed by difficult and painful experiences.

Key vocabulary

Phi Zappa Krappa: a famous poster of American musician Frank Zappa.

king browns: bottles of beer.

Auld Lang Syne: a traditional Scottish song often sung on New Year's Eve.

Q Why do you think Winton presented this story as the introduction to the book's central character, Vic?

Q What kinds of turning points have you started to see in the stories? What might Winton be suggesting about the concept of 'turning'?

'Aquifer' (pp.37–53)

Summary: *The unnamed narrator returns to the suburb of his childhood after seeing news on the television of the discovery of human bones in the local swamp. He reflects upon his upbringing and recalls a particularly traumatic event in his childhood, when he watched a local bully drown in the swamp.*

At the heart of the story 'Aquifer' is the symbolism of water. An aquifer is a layer of rock or sediment that holds and transmits water. In this story, water acts as a representation of the ever-present yet subterranean past. More specifically, the image of human bones being brought up from the swamp acts as a symbol of the past coming back to haunt the main character. Thus, once again, the story links to themes in *The Turning* of how our past affects our present.

Evidently unhappy in his adult life, the narrator speaks in a cynical voice: 'Life moves on, people say, but I doubt that. Moves in, more like it' (p.37). He remains trapped in his past, in particular with feelings of guilt over the way he watched Alan Mannering – a boy who had been bullying him – slowly sink and drown in the local swamp. In the narrator's return to his childhood suburb, the story reflects his quest to confront the demons of his past: 'It's as though I craved discovery, even accusation' (p.52).

On another note, many of the narrator's reflections seem more focused on broad ideas concerning the changing nature of Australian society, and the story may therefore also be read as an allegory for a changing world and how issues of class and race add complications to the way we view our society. While we may try to move on, tension can remain, simmering beneath the surface.

Key point

The past, particularly when it was traumatic, continues to impact the present. We must confront the past if we are to achieve some form of personal transformation and closure.

Key vocabulary

Mariah Carey: popular 1990s pop singer.

BBC voice, 1194: an automated speaking clock accessed in Australia by dialling the phone number 1194.

Poms: British people.

FJ Holden: an iconic Australian car from the 1950s.

Elizabeth Taylor: a British and American actress who played the role of Cleopatra in the 1963 film of the same name.

Q What epiphany does the narrator have at the conclusion of the story? Do you feel this is a positive message or one of defeat and resignation?

'Damaged Goods' (pp.55–65)

Summary: *Gail, Vic Lang's wife, travels to Angelus on weekend trips in an effort to better understand her husband's past. She delves into Vic's teenage infatuation with Strawberry Alison, a girl who rejected Vic's love and eventually died in a car crash.*

'Damaged Goods' builds upon the previous story in exploring the dangers of obsession and the need to face up to the traumas of the past. It appears Vic's obsession over Strawberry Alison has damaged him, as Gail finds him 'weeping over an old photograph and a poem' (p.57). Gail also explains Vic's obsession: having lost his sister to meningitis and his father to alcohol, Vic feels a need to protect others from experiencing similar trauma. As Gail notes, 'Vic will instinctively seek out a victim to defend' (p.58). We see this in his attraction to the 'damaged goods' not only in Strawberry Alison ('damaged' due to a birthmark on her face that explains her nickname) but also in the injured Melanie in 'Abbreviation'.

Yet the story in 'Damaged Goods' goes further, as it also reveals the damage such obsession can cause to one's relationships. Winton repeatedly uses martial imagery through the book to suggest the conflict-laden nature of Vic's relationship with Gail and the world around him. Vic and Gail 'share a sense of having lived under siege' (p.62).

Perhaps, having experienced the trauma of reconnecting with Alison when he finished high school only for her to die that night in a car crash, Vic is unable to revisit the experience. Yet Gail acknowledges that, despite Vic's being 'frozen over, shut down', he and she are 'part of each other's survival' (p.63). This foreshadows the final story in the collection, 'Defender', in which Gail confronts Vic's siege mentality and attempts to find some resolution to their broken relationship. Gail's concluding lines in 'Damaged Goods' seem to reflect those of 'Aquifer': the imagery of 'the heat each of us leaves in our wake' (p.65) is symbolic of the lasting impact of pain that we feel ourselves and radiate out to others.

Key vocabulary

napalm: a highly damaging incendiary substance used by American forces during the Vietnam War.

Vietnam: the Vietnam War, in which Australian forces were involved between 1962 and 1972.

Brandovino and Blackberry Nip: types of fortified wine.

Q Why do you think Winton leaped forward in time so suddenly, from Vic's childhood in 'Abbreviation' to his 'damaged' adulthood in this story?

'Small Mercies' (pp.67–99)

Summary: *Peter Dyson, grieving after his wife's suicide, moves with his son, Ricky, back to his home town, Angelus. He reconnects with his high-school lover, Fay Keenan, and grapples with their shared past and her current addiction issues.*

'Small Mercies' develops the emerging thematic ideas of *The Turning,* with a character returning to his past and confronting his regrets and the events that continue to haunt him. At this point, you may note the way in which Winton has shifted narrative perspectives frequently and has introduced a raft of characters who all face similar issues. In doing so, he seems to suggest the universality of his themes – loss, regret, trauma, confrontation – but he also explores the divergent ways in which individuals react to these experiences.

In 'Small Mercies', Peter Dyson initially opts for resilience and hardiness after his wife's suicide, endeavouring 'to lead a decent, stable, predictable existence' while feeling that he is 'not reconciled but … recovering' (p.68). Yet, as Winton is careful to point out, grief catches up with us: Dyson is struck by 'the sudden ugliness of everything … everything here [is] tainted now' (p.71).

In returning to Angelus, Dyson reconnects, reluctantly, with his high-school girlfriend, Fay Keenan. However, the trauma in the pair's past – an abortion kept secret from Fay's parents – can't be ignored. After

Fay's brutal observation that her parents 'don't know how cold and dead inside' Dyson is (p.97), Dyson realises 'how thoroughly she saw through him' (p.98). No matter how hard he may try, he cannot simply turn away from his past.

Key vocabulary

an icon of a severe Russian Christ: a Russian religious artwork depicting Jesus, used in private devotions.

HT: a car made by Holden in Australia between 1969 and 1970.

tin god: a person who receives unjustified respect.

Q How does Winton encourage readers to sympathise with his characters, even if they are flawed? Consider this in relation to Peter Dyson and Fay Keenan and to the other characters we have met so far.

'On Her Knees' (pp.101–12)

Summary: *Vic, now a twenty-year-old law student, accompanies his mother to her job cleaning an apartment; she is returning for one last time after being fired by the client, incorrectly, for stealing a pair of earrings. They find the earrings and leave them in the kitchen for the client.*

This story, focused on Carol Lang, explores new thematic territory: family bonds, personal pride and class divisions. Following the death of Vic's sister and Bob's abandonment of the family, Vic and Carol have moved back to the city, with Carol taking a job as a cleaner to pay off Bob's debts and keep them 'afloat' (p.101).

The story's central conflict lies between Vic's and Carol's perceptions of moral behaviour. For Vic, the rich client's behaviour in firing Carol is 'unfair, ludicrous, impossible' (p.103), and his reaction is to deny the client the right to one last job. The client, who lives in a community that reeks 'of old money, of posh schools and yacht clubs' (p.105), represents a condescending upper-class society that looks down on the working-class society of Vic's upbringing. For Carol, who is 'proud of her good name' (p.102) and preserves 'her dignity *and* her hourly rate' (p.102), returning to clean the apartment is a symbol of her resilience and self-belief.

The tight domestic space in which the story is set accentuates the conflict between Vic and his mother. The final scene, in which they find the earrings and Vic, after throwing them in the cat litter, places them on the kitchen bench, shows the lesson Vic has learned from Carol: in taking the higher moral ground, we can find greater happiness and self-belief.

Key point

The story ties in to a broader thematic idea with *The Turning*: the way in which family bonds serve to save us – or hold us back – when we are experiencing life's troubles.

Key vocabulary

silvertails: wealthy people.

Electrolux: a brand of vacuum cleaner.

Klee and Kokoschka: Paul Klee and Oskar Kokoschka, early-twentieth-century artists.

objets: ornamental display objects.

Andrew Wyeth: an American artist best known for his 1948 work *Christina's World*.

Germaine Greer, Erica Jong, Betty Friedan: authors associated with second-wave feminism in the 1960s and 1970s.

Kinsey Report: two books that contained the findings of groundbreaking 1940s and 1950s studies of human sexual behaviour; they challenged societal taboos and conventional understandings of sexual norms.

Paul Robeson, Leadbelly [Lead Belly], Dorothy Day, Martin Luther King: an American actor and singer who led the way for African Americans on the stage and screen, an African American folk and blues musician, an American activist and author, and America's most famous civil rights activist, respectively.

Q How does this story reflect others in the collection that explore issues of class divisions in Australian society? Consider 'Aquifer' and even 'Big World' in your answer.

Q How does this story add to your understanding of the 'psychological puzzle' that is Vic Lang's life?

'Cockleshell' (pp.113–32)

Summary: *Brakey, a teenager, finds himself obsessively following Agnes Larwood, a girl his own age, in the small hamlet of Cockleshell. They grow closer until one day the Larwoods' house burns down, killing Agnes' father. In later life, Brakey reflects on his relationship with Agnes.*

'Cockleshell' is another tale of obsession, adolescent angst and the lasting impact of such moments into adulthood. Winton shifts the focus of the story away from the Langs to new characters (the fifteen-year-olds Brakey and Agnes Larwood) and a new setting: Cockleshell, a coastal hamlet. Amid the natural charm of the place, bitter familial conflict resides. Brakey's mother is a broken women, defined by her pessimistic refrain that *'they all leave you in the end'* (p.131). Agnes, a child of British migrants, has a formerly alcoholic and abusive father who has been 'saved' by her mother's religious 'miracle'. But it has left her father 'like a man beaten beyond saving' (p.122), and Agnes feels that 'the house is dead inside, like everything's gone, like even the air is dead' (p.127). Here, Winton taps into the now-familiar themes of families broken apart by suffering and longing, and the failure of adults to adequately look after their children.

Brakey and Agnes' relationship appears as a point of salvation in their grimly static lives. But it is not to be: a house fire that kills Agnes' father (leaving Agnes suspiciously 'calm' and 'serene', p.132) results in Agnes and the rest of her family moving away from the community. Brakey is bereft and confused, even into adulthood. Winton uses the story to explore ideas similar to those found in 'Aquifer', 'Boner McPharlin's Moll' and the Lang narratives – all of which centre on an individual whose profound turning point in life leaves them emotionally scarred.

Key vocabulary

gidgie: a spear traditionally used for catching octopus.

Spartacus and six thousand crucifixions: a gladiator and slave who led a major slave uprising against the Roman Republic in the 1st century BCE; it was defeated, and 6000 surviving slaves were executed.

plimsolls: cheap, everyday rubber-soled shoes.

ten-pound Poms: British people who migrated to Australia after World War II, paying a subsidised fare of ten pounds for the voyage.

Q How does Winton depict adolescent life in this story? Does it align with your own assumptions and experiences?

'The Turning' (pp.133–61)

Summary: *Raelene, a young mother, and wife of the violent Max Leaper, makes friends with a newly arrived couple, Dan and Sherry. Attracted to their simple and clear lives, and intrigued by their religious faith, she gradually finds herself distancing herself from Max, who responds with catastrophic domestic violence. The story ends with Raelene feeling free from Max.*

In this collection of short stories that examine, without any gloss, the brutality and harshness of life, 'The Turning' is the harshest and most brutal, covering issues of domestic violence and rape. Winton shifts perspective once more, to the lives of Raelene and Max Leaper (the latter also featuring in the next two stories) and the setting of White Point, the name imbued with connotations of violence and danger associated with the white pointer, or great white shark.

Raelene is a battler. Living in a caravan park with her young children, she faces a daily threat from her impulsive and unhinged partner: 'He wanted to know where his thermos was and what was for dinner and when the fuck his luck would change' (p.136). Into this claustrophobic life come Sherry and Dan, two born-again Christians who bring Raelene out of her shell and make her feel 'different' (p.143).

Winton uses this scenario to explore a major thematic element in his work: hopes of escape and salvation in the face of traumatic and painful experiences. Sherry's comment about needing 'a little faith' (p.138) and stories of 'David and Goliath' (p.139) touch a nerve with Raelene, who finds herself feeling 'like a kid again' and 'immune' (p.140), a state of equanimity which is short lived. Max, distrustful of her, time and again hurts her violently, and the story ends with a graphic scene of rape.

The story also presents a theme that emerges more in subsequent stories: the dangers of toxic masculinity in an Australian society that accepts, and even values and praises, rugged and physical manliness.

Two important symbols are used in this story to drive its message. First, the landscape, as it does in many of the stories, offers a place of refuge for Raelene. As she walks home at night, she notices that the sky is 'jammed with stars' (p.157), and this sense of a wider, vast landscape provides hope and perspective. The second symbol is found in the 'little cheap-arse snowdome of Jesus walking on the water' (p.155). This seems to symbolise a turning towards religious faith for Raelene. She acknowledges that she needs 'a rescuer' (p.146) and in particular likes how this version of Jesus is 'all man' (p.152) with 'real pecs and a six-pack' (p.155).

At the end of the story, while Raelene experiences horrendous physical violence, Winton seems to suggest she has spiritually and mentally transcended her scenario: 'She was free. She had already outlived him' (p.161).

Key vocabulary

David and Goliath, Jonah and the Whale: Old Testament tales dealing with the power of the underdog and the nature of repentance, respectively.

Givenchy: luxury French perfume.

George W. Bush: American President from 2001 to 2009.

Christ walking on water: a biblical story recounting the miracle of Jesus walking across the water of a lake from the shore in order to reach his disciples, who were crossing the lake in a boat.

Q Winton has been seen as a writer whose main focus is the experiences and issues of modern manhood. What image or images of masculinity do you see emerging in the stories so far?

Q Some critics have suggested that Winton's representation of women in his stories is superficial and problematic. After reading 'The Turning' (and other stories in this collection), to what extent do you agree with this line of argument?

'Sand' (pp.163–9)

Summary: *On a beach trip with their father and his mates, young boys Max and Frank Leaper play in the sandhills. Frank accidentally hurts Max, and Max retaliates by burying Frank dangerously deep under a pile of sand.*

Following on from the depiction of abhorrent violence in 'The Turning', this story gives something of an explanation for the origin of such toxic masculinity: generational layers of poor male influence. Walking symbolically in the 'men's footprints' (p.163), the young Max and Frank desperately try to live up to their gruff and detached father's expectations and demands.

Max, already a dangerous presence with 'side teeth like a dog' (p.165), reacts brutally to a mistake from Frank, burying him with sand. This serves as a symbol for the metaphorical weight that is placed upon Frank, a weight he struggles to escape from. When he does emerge, he feels like he has 'swallowed the earth' (p.169). But rather than expressing anger, he runs after his brother, back to the men, 'apologizing all the way' (p.169).

In this world of masculine bravado, there is no room for weakness. In the next story, we witness the rift that develops between family members when such burdens of expectation are placed upon them. In this story's image of being buried in sand, we see a turning point that – as in so many of this collection's works – is defined by fear and pain.

Q Does this story confirm or change the view of Max that you formed in reading the previous story, 'The Turning'?

'Family' (pp.171–87)

Summary: *Max and Frank Leaper, now in their twenties, go surfing together at White Point. While in the water, they discuss old grievances until Max is attacked by a shark, prompting Frank to attempt to save his life.*

'Family' is, perhaps, the story in the collection that best explores the weight of family and the past that sits on individuals, even as they grow older. In this final episode of the tripartite Leaper narrative, we see the unresolved tension that exists between the brothers. Winton illuminates their inability (perhaps due to their stereotypical masculine tendencies for shutting down) to confront their issues.

The story sees Frank admit to himself that Max has been 'lurking at the back of [his] mind' (p.187). Frank has made more of himself than Max, having been a successful Australian Football League player. But no matter how great his success, Frank realises, he has been 'like some insect [Max] had to squash' (p.182).

The sense of familial resentment plays out in a skilfully constructed setting on the undulating waves of the ocean while they wait for a set. The turbulent nature of the brothers' relationship is accentuated by the 'wave ... twisting on itself' (p.179), and the 'surge of turbulence' (p.185) of the shark attack seems to recall the 'surging, sucking water' that unsettles the narrator of 'Aquifer' (p.47). A subconscious, below-the-surface danger is lurking, waiting to attack when one least expects it.

Key point

Fractured and negative family relationships, especially those driven by toxic masculinity, can be stifling and sit underneath the surface of an individual, causing ceaseless destabilisation.

Key vocabulary

Chuang Tzu (epigraph): a Chinese Daoist philosopher in the 4th century BCE.

Q How does this third Leaper story work with the first two to develop a deeper thematic message?

Q What might Winton be suggesting about masculinity in Australian society through the characters of Frank and Max Leaper?

'Long, Clear View' (pp.189–204)

Summary: *The teenage Vic sits at the window of his home, holding a gun and looking out over the town of Angelus, reflecting on his experiences there.*

Inspired by a true story of Winton's own youth (described in the essay 'The Boy Behind the Curtain'), 'Long, Clear View' establishes Vic as a troubled and anxiety-laden adolescent. The narrative point of view is particularly interesting here: the second-person perspective (for example, 'You narrow your vision', p.190) places us intimately within the closed-off and claustrophobic mind of the young Vic as he struggles to come to terms with the alienation he feels in this small town. Furthermore, the symbol of the gun ('the gravity of a loaded, cocked weapon', p.191), an image of destructive violence and potential calamity, shows the undercurrent of danger that may exist within people who have been outcast from society and the way in which young men in particular may resort to violence as a way of coping with complex feelings.

Regional Australia is not depicted in a good light: 'The place is too small' (p.190). Vic's narrowed vision sees a world in turmoil: 'Down there people are quietly stealing, cheating, lying' (p.201). 'Long, Clear View' shows the burden of responsibility people can feel when their 'clear view' of the world is muddied by the reality around them.

Key point

The story perfectly captures the feelings of confusion and alienation, and the pressures of sudden responsibility, experienced by adolescents as they come to terms with the reality of a world that is tumultuous, corrupt and brutal.

Key vocabulary

trusty: a trustworthy prisoner given privileges.

Status Quo and AC/DC: famous 1970s rock bands.

Tom Jones and Herb Alpert's Tijuana Brass: easy-listening acts who found fame in the 1960s.

Q How does this story represent both life in small-town Australia and the responsibility that falls on adolescents in such places?

Q How does this narrative further illuminate Winton's ideas regarding the impact of adolescence on later life, taking into account what else we now know about Vic Lang?

'Reunion' (pp.205–15)

Summary: *Carol, Vic and Gail head to a family reunion at Uncle Ernie's on Christmas Day. They go to the wrong address, but before they realise their mistake Carol and Gail end up in the pool. Later, they reflect on Bob Lang's absence and the nature of family.*

A joyful story planted in the middle of an otherwise bleak book, 'Reunion' offers a different perspective on themes of family and the impact of the past. The idea of a family reunion, a coming together to share stories and memories and to reforge bonds, evokes mixed emotions, which Winton explores.

From the 'creeping hysteria' (p.209) Gail feels, we understand the trepidation the meeting provokes. Yet, when Carol falls into the pool and is followed by Gail leaping in, the tension breaks. The pool itself is a symbol here, of rebirth and baptism. The story marks a rebirth of sorts, an opportunity for Carol and Gail to overcome the coolness that has separated them: 'We talked and laughed until we forgot the man between us and made some headway' (p.215).

Key vocabulary

Marie [Mary] Celeste: a ship famously found adrift and abandoned in the Atlantic Ocean in 1872.

Q Why might Winton have chosen to narrate this family reunion from Gail's perspective?

'Commission' (pp.217–33)

Summary: *Vic drives into the Eastern Goldfields of Western Australia in search of his father, in order to bring him to see Carol before she dies.*

'Commission' is the first of two stories (with 'Fog' following straight after) exploring Bob Lang's experiences and Vic's fractured relationship with him. In this first story, the journey to a 'ghost town' (p.218) is clearly a symbol for Vic driving back into his past in order to confront the demons that have haunted him since his father left. Trying to overcome his resentment and fury, Vic muses that he 'fears going back to how things were' (p.219).

The irony of discovering that his father has earned the nickname 'Honest Bob' (p.219) is not lost on Vic, given Bob's 'fall from grace' (p.225) during Vic's teenage years. But Winton uses the confrontation between father and son to show how individuals can achieve a form of closure and a turning point if they accept the past and confront it head on.

Vic is 'angry at how sick with love' he feels 'at the very sight' of his father (p.222). But over the course of the evening they spend together, Vic manages to come to some sort of understanding of Bob's experiences. The story ends on a hopeful note of reunion and understanding: 'What he said gave some shape to the misgivings of my youth, the sense that things were not alright around me' (p.231).

Key vocabulary

royal commission: a fictional element in the text, but it could refer to the 2001 Royal Commission into Whether There Has Been Any Corrupt or Criminal Conduct by Western Australian Police Officers, also known as the Kennedy royal commission.

Blundstones: a well-known Australian brand of durable boots.

Q Winton has spoken of being fascinated by hermits and of seeking them out when he was younger. Why do you think he cast Bob as a recluse in this story? What do you make of the setting of a run-down ghost town that houses misfits like Bob?

'Fog' (pp.235–49)

Summary: *Bob Lang, working as a police officer in Angelus, is called to assist a search for some climbers lost in the ranges. He is joined by an inexperienced journalist looking for a story. Together, they find the injured climber, but they are prevented from doing anything more, as fog and then night descend over them, forcing them to wait until daybreak.*

The story is a brilliant piece of exposition, revealing more detail about a character whom we may previously have discounted as a failure and a recalcitrant. So far, the story of Bob Lang has been of a failed police officer turned alcoholic who abandoned his family. In this story, however, we learn that there is more beneath the surface. Winton asks his readers to consider whether there is always more to a story or a life than there seems at first. This is a key feature of the nonlinear, fragmented structure Winton employs; as readers, we gradually learn more about and sympathise more with all the characters and the struggles they face. We also possibly learn to be more accepting ourselves.

The story of a policeman lost in the wilderness is a clear allegory for Bob Lang's sense of being lost morally within the police force. As a 'straight arrow' (p.236), he struggles with the evident corruption in the local police force but is unable to find the 'one honest copper to watch his back' (p.236). He is driven to alcohol: 'This was, he told himself, just a temporary thing' (p.236).

The story thus contextualises Bob within this collection of stories about men struggling to cope with the challenges of life. Building on what we know of the character from the previous story, Winton skilfully engenders sympathy for this honest man who, through no real fault of his own, loses himself in the wilderness.

Key vocabulary

SES: State Emergency Services.

cow-cocky: a small dairy farmer.

Q How do the stories about Bob Lang develop your understanding of both Vic's experiences and the broader themes of the work?

Q Do you feel Winton positions his readers to fully empathise with his characters, or are readers likely to remain critical of the characters' actions and beliefs?

'Boner McPharlin's Moll' (pp.251–92)

Summary: *Jackie forms a relationship with local bad boy Boner McPharlin when she is fifteen and is unfairly given the nickname Slack Jackie as a result. Over time, she drifts away from him, while he becomes involved in drug dealing. After receiving brutal injuries in an attack, Boner becomes increasingly isolated and psychologically unstable. Jackie returns to Angelus as an adult when she receives a call from the police concerning Boner, whose father has died. She discovers disturbing pornographic material at his house. Boner is committed to a mental health unit, and Jackie visits him once a year until his death.*

References to the mythical Boner McPharlin, Angelus' 'local bad boy' (p.251) in the sheepskin jacket, are scattered throughout the other stories. Here, we finally meet him. The idea of Boner being a mythologised figure, heard about but rarely seen, is important thematically for the story. Winton is exploring the nature of reputation, particular in small-town Australia, and how challenging it is to escape the narrative that is formed around us. Once again, we also find there is more beneath the surface.

At the heart of the story is the relationship between Jackie and the older Boner. Boner finds in Jackie a sympathetic friend who provides direction to his drifting existence: 'You're me navigator' (p.266), he tells her. Winton here is perhaps suggesting the way in which men within a toxic environment crave emotional support but turn to stoic silence and violence in their everyday lives.

The story takes a dark turn. In stories such as 'Long, Clear View', 'Commission' and 'Fog' we learn of the drug culture in Angelus and the way in which it is controlled by a corrupt police force; it is in this culture that Boner becomes embroiled. He is brutally beaten one day, with the implication (in 'Commission' and at the end of this story) being that the police themselves are responsible, and he becomes increasingly withdrawn and psychologically erratic. Years later, when his father dies, Boner is found 'cowering in a spud crate behind the shed … suffering from exposure and completely incoherent' (p. 285). Jackie returns to the town when the police contact her, and she visits Boner's abandoned home. She discovers a pile of pornographic magazines. One of the cover pictures has a photo of Jackie's face taped over the model's face: 'I felt robbed, undone' (p.287).

Jackie's narrative is central to the story. Although her reputation has been tarnished by her association with Boner, and despite his increasing instability, she is drawn back to him and this pivotal adolescent experience. Boner both 'appalled and enchanted' (p.252) her, but, bored in the small town of her upbringing, she wanted to have 'something to remember' (p.255). In adulthood, Jackie is still coming to terms with what her relationship with Boner meant. Ultimately, she appreciates that 'in the rush to outgrow the small-town girl I was, I'd left more of myself behind than the journey required' (p.292).

Key point

Significant turning points in our adolescence can be foundational in defining our future identities, even if we never fully understand the profound nature and depth of their influence.

Key vocabulary

Johnny Farnham and David Bowie: a 1970s Australian pop idol and British glam-rock superstar, respectively.

*Airport, M*A*S*H, The Poseidon Adventure:* an airline disaster film, a comedy-drama set in the Korean War and a shipping disaster film, respectively; all American and made in the 1970s.

Ali McGraw [MacGraw]: an American film actress who came to fame in the late 1960s.

Calvinism: a religious theology within Protestant belief systems.

Woodstock: a famous 1969 American hippy festival.

Cleo and Forum: popular magazines that were first published in the 1970s, capturing the zeitgeist of second-wave feminism.

smack: heroin.

Ithaca, Gatsby's place, Golding's island: literary references to Homer's *Odyssey*, F Scott Fitzgerald's *The Great Gatsby* and William Golding's *Lord of the Flies*, respectively. The references suggest places defined by both a sense of wild abandon and revelry and an undercurrent of violence and savagery.

Kharmann [Karmann] Ghia: a type of Volkswagen car produced from the 1950s to the 1970s.

Q How does this story tie in to the themes of toxic masculinity in small-town Australia seen in the other stories?

Q How do you interpret Jackie's ongoing obsession with and attachment to Boner McPharlin?

'Immunity' (pp.293–8)

Summary: *The unnamed narrator reflects on her adolescent attraction to Vic Lang and a brief interaction they once had.*

In puzzling together Vic's life, we are offered a further glimpse into his past and experiences in 'Immunity'. The story is told from the perspective of an older woman reflecting on her unrequited attraction to Vic when they were both younger: 'I knew all about him. I knew he was lonely' (p.295). Her comments about his participation in army cadets ('They're training you for war', p.294) elicit a response from Vic that makes us aware that he has moved on from the anxious teen we saw standing behind a curtain holding a rifle in 'Long, Clear View'. An anecdote he tells about a near miss from a ricocheting bullet is particularly revealing: 'It was kind of like a sign. It made me feel weird. Kind of immune' (p.297).

Winton uses this story to portray an element of resilience and self-belief that we have not previously seen in Vic. Perhaps he needs such qualities to deal with the havoc and tribulations of his experiences.

Key vocabulary

Che Guevara: an iconic Argentinian revolutionary involved in the Cuban Revolution of the late 1950s.

Saturday Night and Sunday Morning: a 1950s British novel by Alan Sillitoe about a young factory worker, focusing on working-class issues.

new war: possibly the war in Afghanistan in 2001 or in Iraq in 2003.

Q Do you feel this story is an important addition to the collection? Consider the collection without it: is it vital in the development of Vic's character arc and the themes of the work?

'Defender' (pp.299–317)

Summary: *Vic and Gail are driving to a property owned by close friends. They discuss the troubles in their relationship and Vic's past, and Gail admits to having had an affair. Over the weekend, Vic does some trap-shooting and gains some perspective on his life.*

The final tale of the collection, 'Defender', is an important piece of the puzzle in the fragmented narrative of Vic Lang. It also serves as a key story that illuminates one of Winton's central themes.

Key point

Individuals who face their past can achieve a sense of closure, salvation and turning, allowing them to broaden their perspectives and save their relationships.

Sickness is a motif in this story. Vic has been struck down with shingles, and the painful viral infection seems to represent his ongoing troubles with the past as they resurface. Gail demands that he deal with it: 'You're stuck, Vic. You won't admit it but you are' (pp.301–2). While Gail praises Vic for being a 'defender' (p.300) of people less fortunate than him as a labour lawyer, her exasperation over their failed relationship is clear, as she claims he is 'like someone under siege' (p.302). This recalls the martial imagery seen elsewhere in the work (e.g. 'Damaged Goods', p.62) that is used to summarise the anxious and tense nature of individuals who have dealt with trauma and havoc in their lives.

The bucolic setting of the final story, with the other couple, Fenn and Daisy, being free-spirited and happy in contrast to the taut and sick Vic and Gail, serves to offer Vic a new perspective on his life. The final scene is a masterstroke in Winton's development of Vic's character arc: standing in a broad valley, with darkness falling around him, Vic fires a rifle at clay targets, finding the activity 'strangely untroubling in its pointlessness' (p.317).

Having engaged in this cathartic act, through which 'nothing got hurt', Vic appears to have reached some kind of epiphany, understanding that it is possible to lead a life less tormented by the past and less focused on the dangers of the world. Winton wants us to end the experience of reading the complex and bleak collection of stories on a positive note, and thus his final image of Vic is a simple and profound statement: 'he was happy' (p.317).

Key vocabulary

neuralgia: pain caused by nerve damage.

Book of Lamentations: an Old Testament text consisting of mournful poems lamenting the destruction of Jerusalem and the exile of the Israelites.

Job: an Old Testament figure who undergoes immense suffering yet maintains his faith in God.

that Tasmanian kid: Australian mass murderer Martin Bryant, who carried out the Port Arthur massacre of 1996.

Q Does the final story successfully resolve, or even attempt to resolve, the issues explored through the collection?

Q How has your view of Vic developed over the course of the book? What can an understanding of this character tell us about the troubles and complexities of real life?

CHARACTERS & RELATIONSHIPS

Vic Lang

Key quotes

'So much of his youth seems to have taken place in an altogether different country.' ('Damaged Goods', Gail, p.62)

'Responsibility is on you now, formless and implacable as gravity.' ('Long, Clear View', p.204)

'You're like someone under siege.' ('Defender', Gail, p.302)

'... he was happy.' ('Defender', p.317)

As the protagonist of the work (if the work can be said to have a protagonist), Vic Lang is the most important character to discuss. In this collection of stories exploring the trials of coming of age and subsequent feelings of regret and pain that last into adulthood, Vic's narrative serves to illuminate the key ideas and the message, in particular, that we need to face our past if we are to find closure in our lives. When writing about Vic, it is important to consider the experiences that most affected him in his adolescence and explore how they impacted his adulthood and his relationships.

We first meet Vic in 'Abbreviation' as a gangly, insecure twelve-year-old on a family holiday. He feels embarrassed by his colourful and overbearing relatives, and his escape along the beach signifies his sense of alienation and dreams of a wider world: 'Out in the calm he dived to the bottom and saw the ripples of the sandy seabed stretching out forever ... He felt free and happy' (p.23).

The first turning point (one of many in his life) is his meeting with Melanie, an older girl with a missing finger, who gives him his first, unforgettable sexual experience – an experience laced with mild violence – that leaves him feeling 'immune; nothing could touch him' (p.35).

However, when we meet Vic again, through the retrospective narrative of 'Damaged Goods', it appears that he struggled to find his identity and sense of self in his small, brutal community. The trauma of being rejected by his high-school crush, Strawberry Alison (who goes on to be killed in a car crash), and the insecurity stemming from the departure of his father (a policeman troubled by the corruption and violence in the local force) lead his wife, Gail, to conclude that he 'lived under siege' (p.62).

The story 'Long, Clear View' develops this element of Vic's character. The claustrophobic, second-person narration depicts Vic standing behind a curtain in his home holding a rifle, filled with anxiety and dread as he reflects upon the violent and chaotic town he lives in: 'Everything you know and all the things you half know hang on you like the pressure of sleep' (p.201).

However, the stories 'On Her Knees' and 'Commission' show a mature Vic trying to get on with his life and even working to defend those around him. Notably, his job as a lawyer connects to the moments when Vic feels a need to help others who are in trouble, a reaction to his own feelings of insecurity and weakness as a teenager.

The final story of the collection, 'Defender', is crucial in understanding Vic's character arc. Vic's marriage is in turmoil and his body is breaking down. Winton seems to suggest that, despite Vic's growing up, marrying and moving away, his past continues to haunt him. But the final image – Vic shooting at clay targets – seems to symbolise a moment in which he comes to terms with this past and finds some form of closure.

A key question to consider in studying Vic's character arc is whether you view him as a failed individual with deep-set flaws or as a man, faced with challenges like anyone else, who does his best to move on and seek happiness and contentment. The ending of the work seems ambiguous: does Vic truly find happiness? Winton seems to want his readers to decide.

Gail

Key quotes

'I'm like some biographer sniffing around in vain for one final, telling detail that will complete the psychological puzzle at the centre of Vic's life.' ('Damaged Goods', pp.55–6)

'Do you realize that every vivid experience in your life comes from your adolescence?' ('Defender', p.302)

Gail, Vic's wife, is an important figure in the book both for revealing more about Vic and for showing how unresolved trauma can negatively impact relationships. We first meet her in 'Damaged Goods', as she visits Angelus in an effort to better understand her distant and detached husband. Vic's obsession with and inability to move on from the past damage his relationship with Gail: 'It's not fun wondering if your husband's love could be another act of kindness … as if you too qualify as his sort of damaged goods' (p.60). This tension comes to a head in the final story, 'Defender', in which Gail admits to having an affair and confronts Vic about their failed relationship, saying, 'I'm just part of some long, faded epilogue to your real life' (p.302).

Carol Lang

Key quote

'She was a substantial person, Carol Lang. I knew she'd endured a lot … Beneath the mildness there was a hard-won pride, a kind of dignity that was intimidating.' ('Reunion', p.206)

Through Carol Lang's character arc, Winton examines themes of resilience and pride and the struggles of individuals in small, working-class communities. Living through the turmoil of a fractured marriage and stuck in an unforgiving community, Carol is depicted as shut-off and bitter: 'Your mother's face is closed' ('Long, Clear View', p.196). Yet Carol refuses to be defeated, and the woman we see in 'On Her

Knees', following her husband's departure and her young daughter's death, is driven by values of pride and self-belief. A 'stickler for order' (p.102), she lives by a 'grin and bear it' (p.110) mentality, which earns the respect of Vic as an adult and sees her survive the challenges of her life with resilience and strength. Her unbridled joy in 'Reunion' and the efforts she makes to reunite Vic and his father in 'Commission' in many ways make her the most heroic character in the book, an understated yet powerful maternal figure who refuses to give up in the face of life's challenges.

Bob Lang

Key quote

'He was Godlike. His fall from grace was so slow as to be imperceptible, a long puzzling decline.' ('Commission', p.225)

Vic's father is a complex character in the text. Seen from the perspective of earlier stories in the collection, he is an absent man, driven to a pitiful state through alcoholism, and he damages both Vic and Carol through his eventual departure from their lives.

Yet through the course of the work, Winton skilfully reveals Bob to be a man with a good heart and a clear moral compass driven to despair by forces outside his control. Speaking of Angelus, Gail notes that it 'crushed' Bob: 'the proverbial straightshooter, [he] became a local joke' ('Damaged Goods', p.59). The catalyst for his failing is the corruption he finds within the local police force, which he initially considers challenging before realising that it poses a threat to him and his family: 'Within months he'd gone from being uneasy to feeling unsafe' ('Fog', p.236).

When we meet Bob again in 'Commission', he is living alone in an outback ghost town, and readers may have already taken Vic's side in seeing the worst in him. However, over the course of this story, we develop a deeper understanding of the challenges he faced, and he gains our sympathy. He was 'stuck, stranded' as 'wheels within wheels' of corruption turned around him (p.230), a victim of a brutal and unforgiving community.

While redemption comes too late, Bob's reunion with Vic at least serves to provide Vic with some closure regarding 'this cloud, this dark thing' (p.230) that has overwhelmed the life of the Lang family. Through Bob's character, Winton asks to us to consider the qualities of bravery and cowardice. Are we capable of challenging the wrongs we see in society, especially when they seem insurmountable? Could we be more forgiving of those who struggle to fight corruption, or will we be more inspired to step forward when the moment demands it? Bob knows how difficult it would have been to challenge the corrupt police who surrounded him, but also seems to regret not having tried harder: 'Cowardice, it's a way of life. It's not natural, you learn it' (p.231).

Max Leaper

Key quote

'In the pub they called him Aggro Max.' ('The Turning', p.137)

Winton is a writer famed for illuminating the pitfalls of masculinity in Australian culture. Max Leaper is a clear target of his criticism. Across the three stories 'Sand', 'Family' and 'The Turning', Winton constructs an image of violent toxicity while providing some background to Max's abhorrent behaviour. Described within 'Sand' as having 'teeth like a dog' (p.165), Max is defined by violent and impulsive behaviour in his childhood. He is unable to show empathy for his little brother, Frank, saying 'he'd kill him if he didn't stop bawling' following an accident at school (p.167). This extends into their adulthood and to Max's abusive relationship with Raelene.

Max clearly had some kind of masculine prowess that appealed to Raelene: 'Right from the start Max was a bloke who didn't muck around' (p.137). But as he grows older and achieves less, the toxic qualities of his character re-emerge. Labelled Aggro Max in the pub where he drinks and with a mouth 'turning down at the sides like a man disappointed' (p.137), Max is representative of a dangerous kind of masculinity characterised by entitlement, failure and inability to act beyond a violent physicality.

Boner McPharlin

Key quote

'Boner McPharlin was the solitary rough boy that country towns produce, or perhaps require. The sullen, smouldering kid at the back of the class.' ('Boner McPharlin's Moll', p.252)

Boner McPharlin inhabits some of the same territory as Max Leaper, being depicted as a sullen, closed and emotionally detached Australian male. Despite his 'truckin stride' and 'sexy insouciance' (p.251), he is an isolated figure, unable to speak even to his friend Jackie on their many drives around town. Yet Winton seems to treat Boner less harshly than Max and may be encouraging his readers to feel sympathy for the young man. He is growing up in an environment that does not allow liberation from the confines of masculine expectations. Not even his best friend knows his real name, Gordon; his nickname has, tellingly, been 'passed from father to son' (p.253).

Before his main appearance, Boner is mythologised in 'Long, Clear View' as 'that wild-looking kid in the sheepskin jacket' (p.192) who 'made bombs and filled condoms with bulls' blood and jacked up teachers' cars' (p.193). With this reputation for misbehaviour, Boner seems unable to escape his fate, even if he wished to. He represents young men who find themselves trapped within a cycle of misdemeanour and havoc, finding that more bad behaviour and chaos is the only way through.

Towards the end of Jackie's narrative, she finds a horrific pornographic image in Boner's hut, which certainly makes us question any sympathy we may have felt towards him. However, on the final page of the story, Jackie's realisation that the police 'played with me, set me against him' (p.292) suggests that this image may have been planted by the police as a way of further isolating him from his only remaining friend. In Boner's plaintive assertion to Jackie that she is his 'navigator' (p.266), we see a young man desperately in need of guidance and direction – direction that is not provided in the rough community of his upbringing.

Raelene

Key quote

'She was free. She had already outlived him.' (p.161)

Raelene is a complex figure. She is both victim and victor, subject to relentless violence from her husband, Max, yet achieving some form of transcendence from her grim situation – although the extent of this liberation is unclear. Raelene is perhaps *The Turning*'s most sympathetic character. She is trapped in grim isolation in the caravan park, unable to escape the coercive control of her jealous and abhorrent husband while trying her best to raise her two children. Despite these challenges, however, she can be filled with self-belief (at one point she realises she is still a 'deadset trophy', p.138) and manages to forge a new friendship.

Attracted to the simple generosity and kindness of Dan and Sherry, Raelene finds herself 'happy but puzzled' (p.141) and 'lifted' (p.143) by their companionship. Eventually, through her discussions with them, she finds some kind of religious salvation, in the form of a symbolic 'little cheap-arse snowdome of Jesus walking on the water' (p.155). Raelene has acknowledged that she can't be alone: 'She needed a bloke ... She needed a rescuer' (p.146). In the masculinised snowdome Jesus, endowed as he is with 'real pecs and a six-pack' (p.155), it appears that Raelene finds a replacement protector.

At the heart of the story is the strength Raelene finds within herself. Feeling as if she has 'climbed from some flaming wreckage an unlikely survivor' (p.159), she rejects a friend's offer of help and looks to a future without Max, knowing she is 'safe from him now, not safe from tonight but gone from him altogether' (p.160). The final ambiguous image in the story, of a pitiful Max smelling 'of death already' (pp.160–1), seems to suggest Raelene's transcendence beyond her miserable life in a future that readers can only hope she achieves.

Other characters

A series of other characters appear within *The Turning*, each apparently defined by and unable to shake off a significant event in their past. These include Jackie, Brakey, Agnes Larwood, Peter Dyson, Fay Keenan, Melanie and the narrators of 'Aquifer' and 'Immunity'. Winton presents them as individuals who have tried and have, to varying degrees, succeeded or failed to 'turn' – to transcend their past, face up to it or move on. Interestingly, he never has these characters meeting (except for those who appear in the same story). Perhaps, in a way, this mirrors the fragmented narrative format of the collection as a whole: most of these individuals struggle to find a sense of belonging to community or to establish lasting connections with others. They are left to move through life, anchored to a past they do not completely understand and adrift in a present that holds little in the way of hope, joy or direction.

While Winton may present his characters at their very worst, experiencing shame, humiliation, hardship and trauma, he is also warm-hearted in his rendering of them. None of these characters is truly awful; instead, Winton carefully constructs them using language that makes us feel the deepest sympathy for them, even while we may criticise their behaviour and life choices.

THEMES, IDEAS & VALUES

Trauma and marginalisation

Key quote

'... the past is in us, and not behind us. Things are never over.' ('Aquifer', p.53)

Disaster is the major element that these stories have in common. Through the course of the book, it appears no one is safe from experiences of trauma and havoc; in fact, these elements seem to be staples of life in Winton's vision of small-town Australia. A shark attack ('Family'), a missing finger ('Abbreviation'), broken legs ('Boner McPharlin's Moll'), a mining death ('Big World') and a drowning ('Aquifer') are just some of the traumatic experiences the characters face. As Gail dryly notes, 'That town, Angelus, wasn't such a quaint place in those days' (p.59).

On the one hand, Winton aims to capture a harshly realistic vision of Australian life, one that doesn't focus on a glamorous urban setting but instead captures the reality of life on the margins, in working-class communities where struggle is a defining and ceaseless presence. Winton populates his stories with battlers, those who through genuine misfortune in life have found themselves marginalised and empty of true hope. This reflects Winton's concerns with class divisions in modern Australian society (Winton 2016) and his ambition to represent those whose voices may be sidelined in Australian literature. This is best seen in the cynical narrative comments made in 'Aquifer' and 'Cockleshell'. In 'Aquifer', the gentrification of the community seems to be achieved at the expense of the landscape: 'As our neighbourhood became a suburb, the bush was heaved back even further on itself' (p.47). In acknowledging that 'everyone's middle class these days', the narrator of 'Aquifer' echoes a cynical sentiment similar to that voiced in 'Cockleshell', when Brakey is 'filled with sudden hatred for all these poncy new bastards overtaking Cockleshell day by day' (p.122). Winton may focus on the damage and destruction in Angelus' surroundings, but in doing so he captures a particular vision of an Australia that does not always get the attention it needs.

On the other hand, these traumatic events, piled on top of each other, seem to have a broader thematic purpose. Winton uses them to suggest that, rather than being anomalies that occur in life, they are in fact the moments that define us. 'Big World' sets the scene with an anodyne form of disaster: Biggie and the narrator's road trip is held up by their broken-down van. Yet this moment is pivotal in their journey of escape, and the story ends with a suggestion of the newfound perspective they find through this experience.

Subsequent stories lean into disaster in more explicit ways and use traumatic experiences to suggest how formative they can be. Melanie's lost finger, the 'Aquifer' narrator's witnessing of a drowning, the impact on Vic of the death of Strawberry Allison – they leave scars, and they are also transforming. Even the brothers' response to the shark attack in 'Family' suggests a fragile bond that may form between Max and Frank, should Max survive. For Winton, it seems, disaster is as ever present as the land and life themselves.

Coming of age

Key quote

'But, you know, all the big things hurt, the things you remember. If it doesn't hurt it's not important.' ('Abbreviation', Melanie, p.26)

Of all the turning points that Winton explores in his work, his key focus remains the turning point of adolescence, a time in life when individuals gain new experience and are exposed to the broader world around them. Winton seeks to capture this in most of these stories and to represent the feelings of both glorious liberation and troubling heartbreak that coming of age entails.

Opening with 'Big World' is a deliberate choice, with the story focused on one of the key rites of passage that Australian youth experience: the end of school. The excitement of personal liberation is clear in the work, with 'feverish … anticipation' (p.1) linked to Biggie and the narrator's dreams of a road trip 'of escape, of pissing up north to find some blue sky' (p.2).

Winton perhaps best captures the excitement of adolescent liberation through the unifying motif of the bonfire at Massacre Point, an event mentioned in 'Big World', 'Damaged Goods', 'Long, Clear View' and 'Boner McPharlin's Moll'. Conveyed in strongly positive tones, the bonfire represents that moment of coming together, of community and warmth fuelled by a shared sense of a future and moving on from the past. In Jackie's description, 'it was the beach at Ithaca, it was Gatsby's place, Golding's island' ('Boner McPharlin's Moll', pp.281–2), the textual references serve to suggest the wild abandon, youthful optimism and a note of foreboding that define coming of age.

However, Winton balances this with more harshly realistic depictions. In doing so, he acknowledges that coming of age is a difficult process characterised by loss (of the past, of youth, of innocence) and by a certain level of trauma and pain. As Melanie surmises in 'Abbreviation', 'all the big things hurt, the things you remember' (p.26). The characters who come of age in Winton's work certainly have things to remember. The narrator of 'Aquifer' remembers that he watched a boy drown yet 'went home and said nothing' (p.46); in 'Boner McPharlin's Moll', Jackie prides herself on her relationship with the town legend yet finds herself ostracised by 'the vile talk behind [her] back' (p.263); and, most significantly, in 'Long, Clear View', Vic is forced to deal with the sudden responsibility placed on him in the edgy town of Angelus and he gradually loses his father, first to alcohol and then to abandonment. This story is probably the most impactful in revealing the pressures of coming of age. While adulthood may appear to be a glorious destination, defined by autonomy and escape, 'Long, Clear View' skilfully shows the burden of responsibility that comes with age: 'Responsibility is on you now, formless and implacable as gravity' (p.204).

Winton does not want us to avoid trauma; instead, he aims to show that it is a vital and expected part of growing up. He encourages his readers, through witnessing it in the worlds of his characters, to better understand how to grapple with it.

Relationships

Key quote

'Family, said Vic. It's not a word, it's a sentence.
Rubbish, said Carol. It's an adventure.' ('Reunion', p.215)

As Leo Tolstoy famously wrote in the opening to *Anna Karenina*, 'Happy families are all alike; every unhappy family is unhappy in its own way.' *The Turning* is certainly filled with diversely unhappy families. Fractured relationships seem to be the norm in the town of Angelus and its surrounds, from the detached parental figures seen in 'Boner McPharlin's Moll' and 'Cockleshell' to the parents who have had to give up on their troubled children, like the Keenans in 'Small Mercies'. *The Turning* rarely depicts family harmony.

But Winton's work does not necessarily pinpoint family dysfunction as the cause of the distress faced by the individuals in his stories; it appears he wishes to explore a different perspective. Indeed, he more commonly reverses the idea, warning his readers that individuals who are damaged or troubled are unable to sustain strong bonds in their *future* personal and familial relationships.

Vic Lang's character arc is a study in the truth of this idea. Acting like 'someone under siege' (p.302), Vic has let his anxiety and fear dominate his worldview, resulting in a fractured and distanced relationship with not only his mother and father but with the person most dear to him, Gail. By having Gail travel to Angelus to 'complete the psychological puzzle at the centre of Vic's life' (pp.55–6), Winton portrays the extent to which those who fail to face up to their past also fail to forge a new future with people in the present.

Pleasingly, in 'On Her Knees', 'Reunion' and 'Commission' we see a far more circumspect Vic, who manages to understand his own issues more clearly. As a result, he is able to build more harmonious and fulfilling relationships with those close to him, as revealed in the positive endings of the stories.

In contrast, some characters never reach this state of emotional breakthrough. The narrator of 'Aquifer' appears to lead a detached and pessimistic existence, held down by his unresolved trauma. In 'Boner McPharlin's Moll', Jackie, lacking meaningful and lasting relationships in later life, ends with the realisation that through her tumultuous relationship with Boner she has 'left more of [herself] behind than the journey required' (p.292). And even Brakey, after his short-lived and unrequited obsession with Agnes Larwood in 'Cockleshell', 'never gets to be much good with women' (p.131). Again, Winton encourages his audience to reconcile past trauma in order to sustain later healthy relationships.

Winton also uses his stories to explore the way in which communities can fail to support individuals and make those who have experienced trauma feel isolated, judged and ostracised. The narrative structure is important here, with the collection comprising loosely connected stories, placed in non-chronological order. Winton shows individuals living in the same coastal region experiencing similar challenges in their lives but rarely interacting with each other in any meaningful way. We thus see them suffering in silence and isolation. The small-town communities of Winton's fictional world have work to do in saving those who find themselves alone and struggling.

Masculinity

Key quote

'Right from the start Max was a bloke who didn't muck around. He never pretended to be what he wasn't.' ('The Turning', p.137)

Why are the male characters in *The Turning* so damaged? What drives them to behave in reprehensible ways? What keeps them from growing into mature, self-controlled individuals with functional relationships and a strong sense of self? These questions are at the heart of Winton's depiction of masculinity in *The Turning*, and indeed masculinity is a theme in almost all of his works. In illustrating, criticising and valorising Australian masculinity, Winton aims to shed light on the experience of men, who are often confined within narrowly defined gender roles and expectations.

More often than not, men in Winton's stories are closed off, defensive and unable to access the language needed to express themselves. They turn to silence or resort to physical violence. Boner McPharlin is a classic case in point. Despite finding some renown as a local troublemaker and 'legend', he is notable for 'his silence, his incuriosity, the way he evaded body contact' ('Boner McPharlin's Moll', p.260). Unable to communicate even with the girl who adores him, Boner is emblematic of a particular stereotype of the Australian male: stoic, pragmatic and physically adept, yet incapable of accessing his emotions. For Winton, emotional reserve is highly problematic: in avoiding dealing with emotions and with the disappointments and challenges in their lives, men in *The Turning* often develop a subconscious pool of anger, unhappiness and pessimism that overflows in the worst ways. For Boner, this is revealed in his dramatic physical and psychological decline, and he ends his life as a crippled man unable to express himself coherently.

The outcome of emotional repression is seen far more abhorrently in the character of Max, initially in 'Sand' and most harrowingly in 'The Turning'. The most truly villainous figure in *The Turning*, Max is an abusive and violent man driven by insecurity and bitterness, who expresses his anger and frustration through physical attacks on those least able to defend themselves, particularly his long-suffering wife Raelene. Like Boner, he has (at least initially) alluring masculine qualities, which drew Raelene towards him in the first place: 'He stared at her like a hungry man, like she was food, and it made her feel powerful' (p.137).

But nothing in Max's character arc redeems his vile actions, and Winton uses him to vilify the very worst in male behaviour: stupidity, aggression and abject violence.

Yet Max is not alone. Raelene's visit to the aptly named Cesspit (pp.158–9) and the description of Max regularly returning home from the local pub 'bloody and sore' (p.137) reveal that he is simply one of many men who embody these characteristics in Winton's small-town Australia. The imagery of the men's vehicles parked in a symbolic 'defensive formation like a bunch of circled wagons from a cowboy flick' (p.158) conveys the underlying hostility that defines them. Raelene witnesses the group 'totally out to it' and watching violent pornography (p.159). While Raelene emerges from this troubling scene at least feeling better about herself and 'fierce' (p.159), Winton has made his point clear: these stereotypes exist; they are not limited to one or two men but are a significant presence in Australian communities.

Yet Winton does not simply depict stereotypical masculine repression and violence. Across the whole collection, almost every man seems to exhibit some form of emotional repression, from the narrator of 'Aquifer' and Peter Dyson to the central character of the whole work, Vic Lang. In 'Aquifer', the narrator leaves the house 'without waking my wife or even leaving her a note' (p.38), while Peter Dyson in 'Small Mercies' is accused of being 'cold and dead inside' (p.97) by his ex-lover Fay Keenan. Dyson struggles to find happiness in his life following the suicide of his wife, although Winton does show him trying to deal with his emotions: 'He knew that things were wrong, that he had to make a change' (p.71).

Vic Lang is perhaps the collection's most complex character study in masculine repressed emotions. Given the tragedies he suffers, it is unsurprising that he becomes a self-defined 'dour bastard … forged in shame and disappointment' ('Commission', p.229). The image of his anxious teenage self hiding behind the curtain 'cradling death in his arms' is one of the most powerful images in the book: a young man who doesn't 'know the first thing about saving himself' ('Long, Clear View', p.309). A recollection of Martin Bryant, the convicted mass murderer, gives Vic a 'chill of recognition … It might have been him at fourteen or fifteen, gun-happy and afraid' ('Defender', p.314). But the final story shows Vic's movement towards a more emotionally secure and self-aware existence, and he becomes a model in many ways for the other lost men in the collection. Winton's point, again, is that men who fail to address their emotional vulnerabilities and who instead turn to stoic silence, emotional detachment and even violence will never progress into the future with hope or a positive sense of a self.

Turning points

Key quote

'[Vic] was forty-four years old but he felt just as helpless. He knew what the boy didn't, that you couldn't keep soldiering on indefinitely. But beyond that, even at this age, he still didn't know the first thing about saving himself.' ('Defender', p.309)

A casual reader might think that *The Turning* comprises only traumatised individuals, broken families, and communities that have failed to unite. However, a central theme in the work is transcendence, or achieving a turning point, and dealing with past trauma. Winton has carefully structured the narrative to show the path an individual may take in order to find closure and salvation.

Vic Lang's character arc is vital in the development of this theme. Troubled by the unsettling drug culture of Angelus and its impact on his father as a policeman, Vic's teenage life seems to be encased in anxiety and fear. These feelings are exacerbated by the death of his little sister and his father's abandonment of Vic and his mother, Carol. As Gail notes, such experiences lead to Vic being 'frozen over' and 'shut down' ('Damaged Goods', p.63). However, Winton inserts significant moments in Vic's life that give rise to a greater understanding of his childhood, and this enables him to face the ghosts of his past and to move on.

The first of these moments takes place in 'On Her Knees'. Furious that his mother has suffered the indignities of not only being accused of stealing but also being asked to clean the client's house one last time, Vic seems unable to comprehend Carol's responses. While working closely with her, however, he comes to the realisation that moving on from anger and resentment is a healthy approach. The final moment of the story, when it appears that 'the very light of day [is] pouring out through her limbs' (p.112), conjures an almost religious image to show Vic's growing appreciation of his mother's dignity and resilience.

This movement towards greater maturity and closure is developed in 'Commission'. Once again, Vic is resentful, this time at having to find his father at the request of his dying mother. But the reunion has a powerful effect upon Vic, making him better appreciate his own adolescence and the challenges his father faced as a moral policeman within a corrupt police force. Perhaps the most affecting image is that of the faded photograph in Bob's house of Vic's 'dead sister hung like an icon' (p.223).

In 'stepping back in time' (p.227) and facing his withered and emotionally weakened father for the first time since he abandoned them, Vic comes to understand that Bob never rejected his love of his family. Their conversation leads to some closure for Vic about his adolescence: 'What he said gave some shape to the misgivings of my youth, the sense that things were not alright around me' (p.231).

The final image of the story seems to be a moment in which Vic gains a new perspective on his family. He sees Bob is ready for the journey back to his wife, looking 'like a man entrusted' (p.233). Vic has glimpsed the man his father was, and the way in which he was damaged by a broken system, and thus comes to terms, to a certain extent, with his own anger at how things played out for all of them.

A final piece of the puzzle appears in the last story in the collection, 'Defender'. With Vic having developed shingles and its accompanying neuralgia, a symbol of his underlying mental torment, Gail stages an intervention. In a beautiful countryside setting, Vic appears to achieve another new perspective, finding a middle ground between the adolescent 'fever' that could have tipped into terrible violence and his subsequent total abstention from even holding a gun ('I haven't fired a weapon for thirty years', p.314). Trap-shooting, he finds, is 'different ... strangely untroubling in its pointlessness' (p.317). The final line, 'he was happy', marks the turning point that Winton has been guiding us towards. Even if such a moment isn't entirely transformative, we can find closure and some form of salvation if we deal with the ghosts of our past.

Landscape

Key quote

'Out in the calm he dived to the bottom and saw the ripples of the sandy seabed stretching out forever.' ('Abbreviation', p.23)

More than anything else, it is Winton's deep understanding and appreciation of the Australian landscape that have inspired his oeuvre. Raised on the expansive coastline of Western Australia and fiercely committed to environmental conservation, Winton pays homage in his works to the beauty of nature and its immeasurable power. Yet landscape is more than a background setting for stories of human endeavour: it is a central character in his works. This is clear in the stories set in and around the embattled township of Angelus, flanked by the vast Western Australian wilderness and the ocean.

The landscape is a presence that many of his characters struggle against or find solace within. On the one hand, Winton's evocations of a vast and powerful natural Australian world (inspired by literary forebears like Patrick White and Randolph Stow) reflect fundamental qualities of Australian identity: freedom, hope, escape, hardiness, resilience, community. This is seen in the beauty of transformative moments in nature, when 'the world suddenly gets big around us, so big we just give in and watch' ('Big World', p.15). On the other hand, his works also capture the other relationship we have with nature that makes us feel lost, powerless, engulfed. This is perhaps best seen in 'Fog', the story of literally getting lost in the wilderness, amid a 'tangled mass of stems and branches' (p.241).

Finally, significantly, Winton's works contain an undercurrent of the violence that Australia's colonial past has wrought on First Nations peoples, displaced and dispossessed of their lands and cultures. The wildness of nature is thus juxtaposed with the newcomers' efforts to restrain it:

> Suburban lots scoured from bushland so that immigrants from Holland, England and the Balkans, and freckly types like us … could build cheap houses … Our homes were new … They were as fresh as we imagined the country itself to be. ('Aquifer', p.38)

DIFFERENT INTERPRETATIONS

Different interpretations arise from different responses to a text. Over time, a text will evoke a wide range of responses from its readers, who may come from various social or cultural groups and live in very different places and historical periods. Responses by critics and reviewers can be published in newspapers, journals and books, both online and in print. They can also be expressed in discussions among readers in the media, classrooms, book groups and so on.

While there is no single correct reading or interpretation of a text, it is important to understand that an interpretation is more than a personal opinion – it is the justification of a point of view on the text. To present an interpretation of a text based on your point of view, you must use a logical argument and support it with relevant evidence from the text.

Critical viewpoints

The Turning has largely been praised for its rich and evocative descriptions of Australian life and the ways in which Winton captures a particularly authentic sense of Australian identity and culture. However, critical reactions have diverged with regards to Winton's depiction of gender. In a 2013 article in *The Sydney Morning Herald*, Nicolle Flint notes:

> While men dominate Winton's fictional world, it is his depiction of women that is of most interest – and concern. It is a depiction that goes near unremarked.

On his works more generally, she writes:

> On one level Winton's women might be construed as literary devices enabling the stories of his slightly bewildered, emotionally repressed Aussie blokes to unfold.
> …

> On another, these female characters appear stereotypical. They 'bother'. What remains most remarkable about Tim Winton's writing, in the context of ongoing allegations of sexism and misogyny, is that the literary left leaves the handiwork of one of our most revered cultural icons unexamined. 'Sometimes,' as Bob Dylan once sang, 'the silence can be like thunder.'

In the #MeToo era, Winton has been cast as out of step with the cultural zeitgeist in his focus on masculinity and apparent sidelining of female characters. Journalist Millie Muroi also explores this in a 2022 article in *The Sydney Morning Herald* in which Tony Hughes-d'Aeth, a professor at the University of Western Australia, suggests that some may think Winton's work is 'too blokey'. In a 2018 interview cited by Muroi, Winton avoided weighing in on the issue. Of the 'feminist critiques', he said: '"[They] puzzled me a bit and anything I say is going to sound defensive, so where can I go there?"' (Alcorn 2018).

In a 2009 blog post, critic Kerryn Goldsworthy situates Winton's lack of strong female characters within a critique of how women are portrayed in literature more broadly, suggesting:

> the masculine world view is still the norm, the feminine world view a lesser variant … the masculine representation of women is still accepted as the truth … (Goldsworthy 2009)

On the other hand, Bridget Grogan is more sympathetic, noting that many men in *The Turning* strive to be better and suggesting it is this ideal of self-improvement that should be the focal point when reading Winton's works:

> At their most complete and tender Winton's men embrace transience and the inevitable loss this entails; simultaneously, they acknowledge the wide beauty of the temporal world and the love of and for others that is both impermanent and yet eternal. (Grogan 2014, p.217)

In a speech given to celebrate the release of his work *The Shephard's Hut,* Winton spoke explicitly about his focus on masculinity in his works, revealing ideas, clearly explored in *The Turning,* of how men are trapped within defined gender roles and expectations:

> Boys and young men are so routinely expected to betray their better natures, to smother their consciences, to renounce the best of themselves and submit to something low and mean. (Winton 2018)

Two interpretations

Interpretation 1: Tim Winton's *The Turning* represents a pessimistic view of Australian life, defined by brutality, selfishness and trauma.

Across the seventeen short stories in the collection *The Turning,* there seems little to be positive about. Death, violence, injury and general havoc are the core elements of life in Winton's depressing small-town Australia, and this critical and pessimistic vision is what drives the narratives. Winton has a distinct style when it comes to illustrating the brutality of life, making it seem commonplace and almost unremarkable. Winton's characters have little to look forward to, as evidenced in the cynical view of the world in 'Cockleshell' ('Nothing lasts. People cheat. They leave', p.116) and the grim forecasting of life ahead in both 'Big World' ('In a year Biggie will be dead in a mining accident', p.14) and 'Damaged Goods' ('Two days of family and then the old man went back out bush and fell down a disused mineshaft', p.63).

Individuals in the stories are defined by the damage and trauma that they are unable to escape. As critic Jem Poster notes:

> Lives dribble away or are brought to premature conclusions ... Even those who seem to have escaped into wider and more promising worlds are tugged back by subtle threads of association. (Poster 2005)

In Gail's detective-like journey into Vic's past, she describes 'a sense of having lived under siege' that seems to be the experience of most characters within the work, growing up amid 'the teenage pregnancies, the roll-call of who died or went to jail before they reached majority' ('Damaged Goods', p.62).

The feeling of being under siege, spread as it is across the whole book, reflects a general lack of hope and the inevitability that individuals will face trauma and drama. Melanie in 'Abbreviation' has accepted this state of affairs with her wise insight that 'all the big things hurt, the things you remember' (p.26), while the narrator of 'Aquifer' has resigned himself to feelings of despair over his traumatic youth: 'Life moves on, people say, but I doubt that. Moves in, more like it' (p.37). It is perhaps Gail, in her position as an outsider, who is most capable of seeing Angelus and its miseries clearly and of understanding their damaging impacts on the residents.

Gallagher notes the contrast between Winton's idyllic settings and the disasters that take place within them: 'The beautiful natural setting ... covers up something that throbs ominously and insistently' (Gallagher 2005). This sense of danger lurking beneath the surface is nowhere better expressed than in 'Long, Clear View'. The image of a boy standing guard at his window with a rifle perfectly encapsulates the fear and anxiety disturbing the interior world of the book's characters. Positioned by the second-person narrative to watch with Vic as the community falls into corruption and violence, the reader can feel the weight of the place: 'Everything you know and all the things you half know hang on you like the pressure of sleep' (p.201).

Gallagher observes that the adults 'stare out in disillusionment as they entrench themselves in their flawed relationships rather than risk moving on' (Gallagher 2005). Interestingly, Grogan links this inability to move on to notions of melancholy drawn from Sigmund Freud's 1917 work *Mourning and Melancholia*, noting how those characters who fail to face up to and mourn their past are stuck in a state of melancholia 'characterised by self-loathing, shame and guilt' (Grogan 2014, p.205). We can certainly see this in the character arc of Vic Lang. In the final story, 'Defender', Gail confronts Vic, saying, 'Every vivid experience in your life comes from your adolescence ... You're trapped in it' (p.302). By the end of this collection of grim, dour stories, we too may feel confined within the miserable and inevitably tragic small-town Australia of Winton's work.

Interpretation 2: In *The Turning*, Tim Winton encourages his readers to see the positive values of seeking closure, preserving strong relationships and finding contentment by facing up to the struggles of our lives.

It is possible to read *The Turning* as an immensely hopeful work that frames trauma and pain as inevitable parts of growing up and offers insight into how we can best use these experiences to become competent and content human beings. For every character who faces hardship and trauma, Winton makes an effort to reveal the hope that lies on their horizon, should they look up and search for it.

Central to Winton's depiction of hope and resilience is his evocation of landscape. From the final moments of 'Big World', in which 'the world suddenly gets big' and the characters 'just give in and watch' (p.15), to the 'hugeness of the sky and the blizzard of stars' in 'Commission' (p.231), Winton continually draws his readers' attention to the transcendent moments that can take place within the natural world. He uses landscape to symbolically suggest that individuals who have faced trauma are not inevitably tied to it and may escape or at least grapple with it in a transformative way. As Gallagher suggests, 'the natural setting sometimes offers characters a poetic glimpse of what life might offer them' (Gallagher 2005), and this glimpse is always one of brilliance and emotional release. For Poster, such 'glimpses provide a necessary counterweight to the stories' harsh social realism, the two elements working together to create a superbly balanced whole' (Poster 2005).

In many ways, Winton is simply trying to alert us to the reality of hardship and then turn our attention to the ways in which we can cope with it on the path to a stronger sense of self. As Grogan states:

> *The Turning* suggests that loss is inherent in character formation, and that one of the transformative aspects of loss is therefore the ongoing construction of the self. (Grogan 2014, p.206)

We see this in the character arc of Vic Lang, who finds himself, at the end of the book, if not fully transformed, at least 'happy' (p.317), given his newly emerging perspective on life.

Another key character is Raelene. Symbolically living within the claustrophobic confines of her caravan, Raelene is trapped within a cycle of brutal domestic violence and the efforts she makes to downplay her injuries and psychological torment when in the presence of friends. In meeting the born-again Christians Dan and Sherry, Raelene is offered a glimpse into what life might be like beyond the closed-in walls of her current existence: 'She came away feeling good about herself' (p.138). As with the other works, landscape plays a central symbolic role in the story. While Raelene appears to find salvation in a very masculine Jesus in a snowdome, it is her moments walking in nature that show the hope and liberation she is starting to perceive:

> She felt woozy for a moment as if she was in the clouds herself and looking down through the gap to see the fires of a thousand desert camps. (p.150)

Winton's focus in 'The Turning', the title piece of the collection, is in fact on the act of 'turning' – achieving some form of transcendence beyond one's experiences and moving towards a more hopeful and promising existence.

Winton accepts that life is hard and can involve great struggle and torment. Yet he does not want to leave us with that as his lasting message. Rather, time and again in these stories, characters are offered a new perspective, and for many, it appears that the journey ahead is promising.

QUESTIONS & ANSWERS

This section focuses on your own analytical writing on the text, and gives you strategies for producing high-quality responses in your coursework and exam essays.

Essay writing – an overview

An essay on a literary work is a formal and serious piece of writing that presents your point of view on the text, usually in response to a given topic. Your 'point of view' in an essay is your interpretation of the meaning of the text's language, structure, characters, situations and events, supported by detailed analysis of textual evidence.

Analyse – don't summarise

In your essays it is important to avoid simply summarising what happens in a text.

- A **summary** is a description or paraphrase (re-telling in different words) of the characters and events. For example: 'Macbeth has a horrifying vision of a dagger dripping with blood before he goes to murder King Duncan'.
- An **analysis** is an explanation of the real meaning or significance that lies 'beneath' the text's words (and images, for a film). For example: 'Macbeth's vision of a bloody dagger shows how deeply uneasy he is about the violent act he is contemplating, and conveys his sense that supernatural forces are impelling him to act'.

A limited amount of summary is sometimes necessary to let your reader know which part of the text you wish to discuss. However, always keep this to a minimum and follow it immediately with your analysis of what this part of the text is really telling us.

Plan your essay

Carefully plan your essay so that you have a clear idea of what you are going to say. The plan ensures that your ideas flow logically, your argument remains consistent and you stay on topic. An essay plan should be a list of **brief dot points** covering no more than half a page.

- Include your central argument or main contention – a concise statement of your overall response to the topic.
- Write three or four dot points for each paragraph, indicating the main idea and evidence/examples from the text. In your essay you will need to expand on these points and analyse the evidence.

Structure your essay

An essay is a complete, self-contained piece of writing. It has a clear beginning (the introduction), middle (several body paragraphs) and end (the last paragraph or conclusion). It must also have a central argument that runs throughout, linking each paragraph to form a coherent whole. See examples of introductions and conclusions in the 'Analysing a sample topic' and 'Sample answer' sections.

The introduction establishes your overall response to the topic. It includes your main contention and outlines the main evidence you will refer to in the course of the essay. Write your introduction *after* you have done a plan and *before* you write the rest of the essay.

The body paragraphs argue your case. They present evidence from the text and explain how this evidence supports your argument. Each body paragraph needs:

- a strong **topic sentence** (usually the first sentence) that states the main point being made in the paragraph
- **evidence** from the text, including some brief quotations
- **analysis** of the textual evidence, with **explanation** of its significance and how it supports your argument
- **links back to the topic** in one or more statements, usually towards the end of the paragraph.

Connect the body paragraphs so that your discussion flows smoothly. Use some linking words and phrases such as 'similarly' and 'on the other hand', though don't start every paragraph like this. Another strategy is to use a significant word from the last sentence of one paragraph in the first sentence of the next.

Use key terms from the topic – or synonyms for them – throughout, so the relevance of your discussion to the topic is always clear.

The conclusion ties everything together and finishes the essay. It includes strong statements that emphasise your central argument and provide a clear response to the topic.

Avoid simply restating the points made earlier in the essay – this will end on a very flat note and imply that you have run out of ideas and vocabulary. The conclusion should be a logical extension of what you have written, not just a repetition or summary of it. Writing an effective conclusion can be a challenge. Try using these tips:

- Start by linking back to the final sentence of the second-last paragraph, rather than leaping to your main contention straight away – this helps your writing to flow.
- Use synonyms and expressions with equivalent meanings to vary your vocabulary. This allows you to reinforce your line of argument without being repetitive.
- When planning your essay, think of one or two broad statements or observations about the text's wider meaning. These should be related to the topic and your overall argument. Keep them for the conclusion, since they will give you something 'new' to say but still follow logically from your discussion. The introduction will be focused on the topic, but the conclusion can present a wider view of the text.

Essay topics

1. How has Winton captured a distinctly Australian cultural identity in *The Turning*?
2. In what ways has Winton used the fragmented narrative structure of *The Turning* to explore shared human experiences?
3. How has Winton used symbolism to connect the stories and ideas within *The Turning*?
4. "… the past is in us, and not behind us. Things are never over." ('Aquifer', p.53)
   To what extent does this reflect your understanding of the nature of the past in *The Turning*?
5. 'Despite Vic's damaged character, he remains an emblem of how we can move on and make progress as individuals.'
   To what extent do you agree?
6. 'There are no heroes, only survivors.'
   Discuss this idea with reference to the characters in *The Turning*.
7. "What [Bob] said gave some shape to the misgivings of my youth, the sense that things were not alright around me."
   ('Commission', p.231)
   Reflecting on the quote above, how does *The Turning* represent characters in a quest for understanding?
8. 'Great literature allows us to see the world as more complicated, more fraught and more challenging than we might previously have thought it to be.'
   Discuss this idea with close reference to *The Turning*.
9. 'Men in Winton's works are unable to grapple with the complexity of life and instead resort to emotional repression and physical brutality.'
   To what extent does this view align with your understanding of the male characters in *The Turning*?
10. 'Misogyny, like racism, is one of the great engines of intergenerational trauma.' (Winton 2018)
    To what extent do you feel that misogyny is at the heart of the stories and the experiences of the characters in *The Turning*?

11 'Our identity is forged by the challenges we face.'
To what extent does *The Turning* support this idea?

12 'Relationships are fundamental in shaping our character.'
Discuss this idea in relation to *The Turning*.

13 'Hope is humanity's most vital need.'
Evaluate this idea in relation to your understanding of *The Turning*.

Analysing a sample topic

'Relationships are fundamental in shaping our character.' Discuss this idea in relation to *The Turning*.

Firstly, ensure you fully understand the statement by highlighting key terms: 'relationships', 'fundamental' and 'shaping our character'. Then expand on these terms to deepen their meaning. For example, 'relationships' could mean any form of human connection: family, friends, community, lovers, even relationships with the places where we live and work. 'Fundamental' implies vital, foundational, important or influential. And finally, 'shaping our character' suggests identity, the process of finding out who we are, what motivates us and what defines us. So, rephrased, the statement suggests that a range of relationships are vital in forming our identities.

It is always useful to work out whether you fully agree with the statement and how you might offer an alternative idea at some point in your essay. You might look for a 'however' option in response to the question (e.g. *'However, individuals can maintain a strong character regardless of the influence of relationships'*). You can also rearrange the statement to see if you can formulate another way of answering it (e.g. *'Relationships may impact our character, but could character also shape our relationships?'*). Try not to fully disagree with a topic (e.g. *'No, relationships have no impact on our character'*), but do consider whether other elements could be introduced to expand the range of points you can argue.

Brainstorm and gather your ideas in clear, distinct subtopics. These will eventually become the different points you will explore in your body paragraphs. For example:

- Family relationships are foundational in shaping our sense of self as we grow up.
- The relationships we form in our communities, with friends and loved ones, shape our lives and the decisions we make.

Once you have your ideas, pick out the best ones, gather your evidence (quotations) to ensure you can fully prove these ideas, and finally, construct your topic sentences and consider the order in which you will present them. Below is a sample of how you could answer this question.

Sample introduction

Give a clear response to the statement. Introduce your text and the various ideas you will prove. Connect back to the question.

> Relationships are foundational in defining who we are and shaping our sense of self as we move through life. Tim Winton's work *The Turning* considers the profound impact that relationships have on individuals and how they can have a lasting influence on people's lives and values. In particular, Winton explores the foundational way that family and community relationships shape individuals' values and beliefs long after they have grown up and moved away from those formative connections. Yet, Winton is also careful to illuminate how the reverse of this statement is true: individuals' characters can strongly impact their relationships. If characters have been shaped by trauma and loss, this can have a negative impact on individuals' ability to build robust relationships later in life.

Body paragraph outline

Paragraph one: Winton explores the strong role that family relationships have in defining and shaping individuals' characters.

- Draw on material from Vic's narrative, with the influential roles of Carol and Bob in shaping his character.
- Link to other characters, especially exploring experiences of family pressure, feelings of alienation and the impact of parental absence. Characters to discuss include Agnes Larwood, the Leaper brothers and Boner McPharlin.

Paragraph two: Winton develops this idea by considering the profound influence of relationships formed in communities.

- Explore the nature of friendship, of being outcast and of peer pressure in small communities, linking to 'Big World', Jackie in 'Boner McPharlin's Moll' and the narrator of 'Aquifer'.
- Consider how such influences remain with individuals for life, using Peter Dyson, Vic and Jackie as examples.
- Discuss how obsessive and unhealthy relationships can leave a lasting mark on people's psyches. Examples include Jackie, Vic and Brakey. Raelene's relationships with Max, Dan and Sherry are also worth exploring, although they are more complex and their long-term effects on Raelene are not described.

Paragraph three: Winton suggests that individuals' past experiences and character flaws are fundamental in shaping their relationships, especially those later in life.

- Consider Winton's idea that those with trauma in their past struggle to maintain strong relationships.
- Look at broken family relationships, particularly Vic's fraught relationship with Gail and possibly the Leaper brothers.
- Discuss the characters who try to mend broken relationships, overcoming their damage and finding a way through – for example, Peter Dyson, Vic and Bob.

Sample conclusion

We are defined by those around us. In some cases, we have little choice in the matter: in *The Turning*, Winton explores how family exerts a profound influence on who we are and who we grow up to be. Similarly, he suggests that relationships we seemingly make by choice – those with friends, lovers and community members – also shape us, inform our values and have a lasting impact. But in considering the strong role of relationships on our characters, Winton also makes us aware of the influence that our characters have on our relationships. He encourages his readers to forge a strong sense of self in order to move forward and have meaningful and resilient relationships in the future.

SAMPLE ANSWER

'Great literature allows us to see the world as more complicated, more fraught and more challenging than we might previously have thought it to be.' Discuss this idea with close reference to *The Turning*.

Great literature challenges its readers by exposing them to worlds beyond their own experiences, forcing them to see life as more complicated and fraught than previously assumed. *The Turning,* Tim Winton's 2004 collection of interwoven short stories, skilfully exposes readers to the difficult lives of those in small-town Australia who face daily hardship and struggle through seemingly endless challenges. In representing the complex, imperfect reactions his characters have to such challenges, Winton allows his readers to see the world in a new light. However, he moves beyond a purely pessimistic vision of the world by also helping readers to comprehend how they might find hope and salvation in the face of life's challenges.

Great literature allows us to see the brutality and challenges that are an essential part of life, revealing the world to be a perilous place. In the town of Angelus, complexity is a way of life, and Winton uses this fictional world to depict a version of Australia in which hardship is the norm. Gail's dry observation about Angelus in 'Damaged Goods', 'the teenage pregnancies, the roll-call of those who died or went to jail before they reached majority' (p.62), perfectly summarises the fraught environment in which the stories take place. Indeed, Winton confronts his readers with a working-class Australian life of almost daily grapples with hardship and conflict. This 'altogether different country' is best captured in 'Long, Clear View', which uses a claustrophobic second-person narration. The paranoid teenage Vic Lang watches as his town succumbs to a drugs epidemic, with the story running through a catalogue of catastrophes from arson and drownings to car crashes, brutal beatings and suicides. The town and its surrounds, where the 'scarred and broken-toothed' blue-collar workers live in symbolically named locations like White Point, Thunder Beach and Massacre Point, seem to embody an underlying ever-present threat of violence and chaos. Alongside this, it appears even the family unit has been fractured, with the tension captured perfectly in Agnes Larwood's comment that 'even the air is dead' within her cold and broken home. Thus, across the course of the seventeen bleak narratives, Winton provides his readers with an inside look at a world defined by difficulties.

Furthermore, literature enables us to see how fraught and complicated life can be if we are not equipped to handle the challenges that are thrown our way. The characters in *The Turning* struggle with the trauma in their lives. Almost every adult character in the work – from the narrator of 'Aquifer' and Raelene in 'The Turning', to Frank Leaper and Vic Lang, the central character of the collection – is characterised as trapped and paralysed in their life, unable to move on or confront the past. Even the narrator of 'Big World', who expresses a genuine desire to move beyond the 'other poor stranded failures who stayed in Angelus', is brought back to reality when his road trip ends in failure. Some characters are held back by the weight of family expectation. Frank, the promising footballer whose career becomes 'unstuck', articulates this best. In reflecting upon why his career failed, he reaches the realisation that it was his brutal brother, Max, who metaphorically 'poisoned him', reducing any ability he had to succeed by 'lurking at the back of [his] mind'. Others, like Vic, are weighed down by the unresolved issues of their childhood, 'frozen over, shut down' in later life. Winton skilfully uses the olfactory imagery of Angelus' whaling industry in a description of Vic: 'Unspoken worries hung over him like the omnipresent stink of the harbour'. We perhaps see the state of paralysis best in the narrator of 'Aquifer'. With his mind metaphorically 'travelling in loops and ellipses', he comes to the realisation that 'things are never over', especially if those things are confused and challenging.

However, Winton moves beyond a static representation of a hazardous, complex world to convey a positive message regarding how we can deal with life's challenges. Images of escape recur in the text and are often tied to symbolically vast landscapes that offer characters hope and reprieve from their difficulties. From the 'ripples of the sandy seabed stretching out forever' in 'Abbreviation' to the 'hugeness of the sky' in 'Commission', the landscape offers many characters a glimpse of something beyond their entrapped lives. A strong, resilient woman, Marjorie Keenan simply feels 'grateful for small mercies' amid the struggles of her family life. Carol Lang holds on to a profound sense of personal dignity, 'proud of her good name'. Most significant, though, is Vic's journey through the stories as he endeavours to overcome his paralysis and find closure and salvation. Having seen him grow from an anxious teen to a distracted labour lawyer, readers may look to Vic as an example for how they might tackle the inevitable challenges they face. While he is not perfect, his burgeoning understanding of himself and his courage in confronting his past and finding 'some shape to the misgivings of [his] youth' signal a way through. The final, symbolic image of the book – 'darkness had fallen around him and he was happy' – suggests that closure and contentment can be found if we seek it and work through the challenges that come our way.

Hardship may be one of life's constant and foundational elements, and great literature acts to expose us to this reality. From the trials of adolescence to the challenging nature of adult relationships, Winton shows life to be fraught with moments of havoc, danger and heartache. His collection of short stories forces readers to confront these experiences and accept them. Yet hope exists, and, while we may find ourselves confronted by such complications as are portrayed in literature, we can also see that there is a way through. By looking to these literary worlds and the characters within them for guidance and optimism, we too may navigate a challenging but thrilling and fulfilling life.

REFERENCES & READING

Text

Winton, T 2006, *The Turning*, Picador, Sydney.

References

Alcorn, G 2018, 'Tim Winton: being called a misogynist stings a bit', *The Guardian*, 26 June, https://www.theguardian.com/books/2018/jun/26/tim-winton-most-of-the-men-in-my-books-are-doing-badly

Flint, N 2013, 'Misogyny lurks in Winton's world of fiction', *The Sydney Morning Herald*, 1 August, https://www.smh.com.au/opinion/misogyny-lurks-in-wintons-world-of-fiction-20130731-2qze8.html

Gallagher, S 2005, 'Winton's overlapping stories analyze disillusionment but don't disappoint' (review of T Winton, *The Turning*), *Antipodes*, vol. 19, no. 2, pp.220–2.

Goldsworthy, K 2008, '*Breath*, by Tim Winton, and the May issue of *Australian Book Review*', *Australian Literature Diary*, 3 May, http://austlit.blogspot.com/2008/05/breath-by-tim-winton-and-may-issue-of.html

——2009, 'Biblical worldview legitimised: Australian feminist icon turns in grave', *Still Life with Cat*, 18 June, http://stilllifewithcat.blogspot.com/2009/06/biblical-world-view-legitimised.html

Grogan, B 2014, 'The cycle of love and loss: melancholic masculinity in "*The Turning*"', in L McCredden & N O'Reilly (eds), *Tim Winton: Critical Essays*, UWA Publishing, Crawley, pp.199–220.

Ley, J 2008, '*Breath* by Tim Winton' (review), *Australian Book Review*, no. 301, https://www.australianbookreview.com.au/abr-online/archive/2008/149-may-2008-no-301/5575-james-ley-reviews-breath-by-tim-winton (subscription required)

Muroi, M 2022, 'Too "blokey" and cliched? Why Tim Winton has become one of our most divisive authors', *The Sydney Morning Herald*, 4 June, https://www.smh.com.au/culture/books/too-blokey-and-cliche-why-tim-winton-has-become-one-of-our-most-divisive-authors-20220520-p5an2u.html

Nicols, C 2022, 'Tim Winton on a life of accidents, successes, and the business of "useless beauty"', *Big Weekend of Books* (radio broadcast), ABC, https://www.abc.net.au/listen/programs/big-weekend-of-books/tim-winton-on-a-life-of-accidents-successes-useless-beauty/14003096

Poster, J 2005, 'Big dreams' (review of *The Turning*), *The Guardian*, 2 April, https://www.theguardian.com/books/2005/apr/02/featuresreviews.guardianreview23

The Royal Academy Podcast Team 2016, 'Short stories with Tim Winton', 23 March, available at https://open.spotify.com/episode/1p3R8kJDokNXkMfzA2OIUd?si=CbKf4SM0Rlu6mZ8HW8Bvng

Winton, T 2015, *Island Home*, Penguin, Melbourne.

——2016, *The Boy Behind the Curtain*, Penguin, Melbourne.

——2018, 'About the boys: Tim Winton on how toxic masculinity is shackling men to misogyny', *The Guardian*, 9 April, https://www.theguardian.com/books/2018/apr/09/about-the-boys-tim-winton-on-how-toxic-masculinity-is-shackling-men-to-misogyny